BUG LAB FOR KIDS

FAMILY-FRIENDLY ACTIVITIES FOR EXPLORING THE AMAZING WORLD OF BEETLES, BUTTERFLIES, SPIDERS, AND OTHER ARTHROPODS

JOHN W. GUYTON, ED.D.

QUARRY

Brimming with creative inspiration, how-to projects, and useful information to enrich your everyday life, Quarto Knows is a favorite destination for those pursuing their interests and passions. Visit our site and dig deeper with our books into your area of interest: Quarto Creates, Quarto Cooks, Quarto Homes, Quarto Lives, Quarto Drives, Quarto Explores, Quarto Gifts, or Quarto Kids.

First Published in 2018 by Quarry Books, an imprint of The Quarto Group, 100 Cummings Center, Suite 265-D, Beverly, MA 01915, USA.
T (978) 282-9590 F (978) 283-2742 QuartoKnows.com

Quarry Books titles are also available at discount for retail, wholesale, promotional, and bulk purchase. For details, contact the Special Sales Manager by email at specialsales@quarto.com or by mail at The Quarto Group, Attn: Special Sales Manager, 401 Second Avenue North, Suite 310, Minneapolis, MN 55401, USA.

10 9 8 7 6 5 4 3 2 1

ISBN: 978-1-63159-354-3

Digital edition published in 2018

Library of Congress Cataloging-in-Publication Data available.

Interior Design: Kathie Alexander
Page Layout and Design: *tabula rasa* graphic design
Photography: John W. Guyton and Shutterstock
Illustration: Mattie Wells on page 33

Printed in China

MIX
Paper from responsible sources
FSC® C101537

Dress appropriately when preparing to collect insects and use bug repellents according to label directions. Some bugs are dangerous—get to know the ones in your area that are and do not touch or handle them. If you have a severe allergic reaction such as difficulty breathing (anaphylaxis) or are bitten by a dangerous insect, seek medical attention immediately. The publisher and author assume no responsibility for bites, stings, or any other injuries that may occur while performing these labs.

This book is dedicated to Peggy Guyton,
my wife and partner in life's journey.

CONTENTS

INTRODUCTION

Many young people are naturally curious about and attracted to bugs. Parents and teachers can take advantage of this natural curiosity to sustain students' interest in science and provide an avenue through which they can explore their world.

A NOTE TO PARENTS AND TEACHERS

Insects and other arthropods outnumber all other animals combined. *More than 95 percent of all animals may be insects!* Insects are incredibly successful, and research suggests they have at least a 450-million-year record of survival on a changing and periodically hostile planet! The pocketsize critters even survived the dinosaurs in, essentially, their current form!

There is obviously a lot we can learn from insects. Insects are our principal competitor for food, and we cannot survive without their beneficial services. Arthropods are found everywhere; they are our most common encounter with wildlife. They are essential in pollination, recycling nutrients, and the production of many useful products. They are a critical link in the web of life.

Our interactions with insects can nurture curiosity and enable youth to develop a realistic and balanced relationship with arthropods, instead of the unnecessary and uneducated frightened reactions.

The Entomologists of Tomorrow

The fascination that young entomologists—people who study bugs—have for arthropods is the beginning of an adventure of discovery that can last a lifetime. Wherever they roam there will be new arthropod adventures awaiting. This curiosity is infectious and, if nurtured, will provide a healthy use of leisure time. They will quickly become *the* entomologist in their families and peer groups, and this often encourages advanced study. On their arthropod adventures, they will encounter legions of entomologists who will find their curiosity inspiring and who will patiently answer their questions, share their interest, and guide them. Young entomologists' knowledge will amaze their teachers and earn their respect.

It has been a privilege to watch so many young entomologists pass through our programs at Mississippi State University, growing intellectually and enjoying a healthy use of their leisure time.

PREPARING FOR BUG ADVENTURES

DRESS TO COLLECT

Dressing appropriately for a collecting trip helps ensure your encounters with arthropods are successful. Bites and stings, especially from mosquitoes and ticks, are easily minimized by wearing the proper collecting outfit and/or using insect repellent. High rubber boots, long-sleeved shirts, long pants, and veils are appropriate for excellent protection.

STEP 1: Gather your collecting clothes. It is best to wear long pants and a long-sleeved shirt.

STEP 2: Put on your boots and tuck your pant legs into the boot tops. Loosely wrap duct tape around your pants several times, at the top of each boot, to secure your pants to your boots. On the last wrap, flip the tape, sticky-side out, to collect pests trying to crawl up your pant legs. If you're collecting in the woods, grasslands, or prairie and wearing shoes instead of boots, securely tape your pant legs to your shoes, turning the tape for the last wrap sticky-side out. *Sandals are not appropriate collecting gear.*

STEP 3: Spray any exposed areas with insect repellent (do not spray it on your face, though).

STEP 4: In the late afternoon and evening, wear a net or veil over your head to protect you from mosquitoes and biting midges.

STEP 5: Check the duct tape after each trip to see if it collected ants, ticks, or redbugs.

STEP 6: After every collecting trip, carefully check yourself for ticks, or have an adult help you (see page 16).

Wearing proper collecting clothes—long pants, a long-sleeved shirt, high rubber boots, a cap or hat, plus duct tape, insect repellent, and a net or veil—will help make your encounters with arthropods both safe and successful.

BUG SCIENCE

Entomologists seek places where insects are abundant, so appropriate attire is very important. For example, an important consideration if working with bees is not to dress in contrasting colors, like black and white. A light-skinned beekeeper with a black watchband can expect bees to sting on the wrist. Similarly, a white shirt on darker skin will attract stings to the point of greatest contrast.

ORGANIZE A COLLECTING KIT

Collecting insects safely requires specialized equipment and techniques. In addition to proper collecting clothes (see page 10), including a veil to protect you from bites, consider which materials from the following list will serve you best, depending on where you are collecting, your collecting strategy, and your goals.

- Aspirator, for small bugs (see Lab 8, page 42)
- Beat sheet, for bugs in shrubs and small trees (see Lab 9, page 44)
- Black light, for night collecting (see Lab 11, page 48)
- Camera
- Critter keeper, for live specimens
- Forceps or tweezers, for picking up biting or stinging arthropods
- Insect field guide or identification book
- Insect net (see Lab 4, page 28)
- Insect repellent
- Non-acetone nail polish remover (ethyl acetate), for dry collecting jar
- Pencil
- Pitfall traps (see Lab 10, page 46)
- Rubbing alcohol (isopropyl alcohol, 60%), for wet collecting jar
- Shoulder bag, to carry your kit

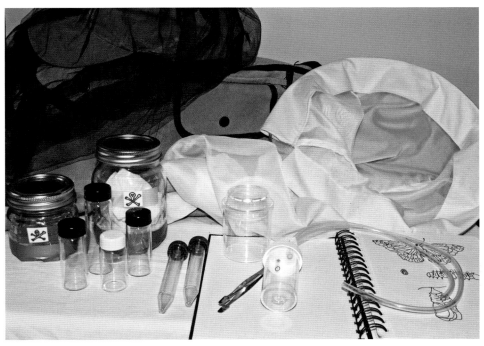

Some essential collecting kit items.

- Trowel, for digging a pitfall trap or digging into rotting logs
- Vials or pill bottles
- Wet and dry collecting jars (see Lab 7, page 36)
- Your field notebook

A well-organized collecting kit enables you to quickly charge your dry and wet jars and head for the field. Occasions regularly arise when an interesting insect shows up and, if you are prepared, you can collect it. You may want to take all your supplies with you, but it is not necessary—carry just what you need.

STEP 1: For each outing, charge your collecting jars and pack your shoulder bag with your essential equipment. Take only what you think you will need.

STEP 2: Go on your collecting trip and try out your kit.

STEP 3: Afterward. reflect on your trip and review any notes you made in your field notebook (see page 12). Do you need to practice some of your collecting skills?

START A FIELD NOTEBOOK

Scientists make careful observations and record them in their field notebooks. Your field notebook will become your faithful companion as you record your arthropod adventures, and a place for you to reflect on all you've learned and observed.

Some considerations for using your field notebook include:

Any book with blank pages is suitable. It could be spiral bound or hard bound.

Make entries with a pencil, as ink smears if the notebook accidentally becomes wet.

Record as much information as possible to document each event, including:

- Date
- Time of day
- Weather conditions
- Arthropods collected or observed
- Type of plant on which you observed the insect
- Type of insect activity observed
- Names of those accompanying you
- Conclusions from your research
- Plans for using this information in future experiments

In documenting experiments you will benefit from a standard format, including:

- Control and experimental groups
- Hypotheses or statements about the possible outcomes
- Control measures
- Results
- Other possible influences on outcomes

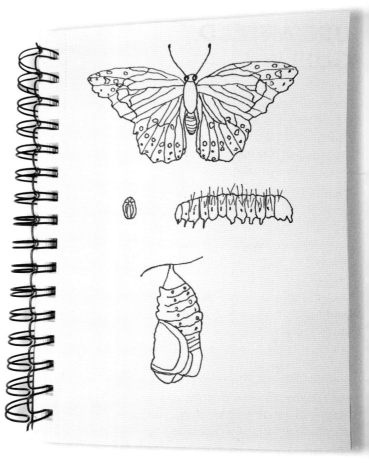

Your field notebook is the place to record your observations, collecting trips, and experimental procedures. These notes are of the greatest importance to scientists.

USE A FIELD GUIDE

You will enjoy using a field guide with this book. Once you have identified the insect or other arthropod you have collected using the field guide, the internet can provide a wealth of additional information.

Choose a field guide that contains insects and other arthropods, including centipedes, millipedes, spiders, scorpions, mites, etc. It should be a recent publication and include insect range maps.

Look at pictures of insects in a field guide, including beetles, moths, and butterflies; bees, ants, and wasps; flies; crickets; dragonflies; roaches; termites; and praying mantes. Notice they are in groups with similar bugs called *orders*. You can use the field guide to add the order and genus species, if you wish, to your notes about each insect in your field notebook.

A young entomologist consults a field guide

FIRST AID: BITES AND STINGS

Insects and arthropods have many predators, so they have developed a variety of defense measures to protect themselves, including biting, stinging, and spraying chemicals. Fire ants bite to grab hold and then they sting you! Mosquitoes are of particular concern because they carry diseases they transmit by biting people. Kissing bugs—with their cone-shaped heads and red or yellow stripes around their abdomens—harbor a parasite that causes Chagas disease. They feed on blood at night, preferring areas around the mouth or eyes. Because they are a parasite, DO NOT handle them.

Some basic tips:

Be prepared. Dress appropriately when preparing to collect insects and use bug repellents according to label directions. When using good collecting techniques, it is not necessary to hold live arthropods. *Best practice is to use your net or trap to collect all insects and transfer them directly into a collecting jar without touching them.*

If you get stung by a bee or wasp, clamp a hand over the sting site and head inside to treat the sting. Clamping your hand over the sting site is important because the stinging insect may have left a chemical "tag" to attract other insects to attack the same site.

As soon as you are inside, smell the spot where you were stung. Does it smell like

BUG SCIENCE

The terms *venomous* and *poisonous* are often used interchangeably and incorrectly. *Poison* is something you drink or eat. Many arthropods are *venomous*, meaning they inject venom in their prey or attackers. There are a wide variety of venoms used by arthropods. There are biting and stinging arthropods, stinging caterpillars, and tarantulas that can bite or kick *urticating* (irritating, stinging) hairs off their abdomens. Insect saliva contains anticoagulants and enzymes that can cause local irritation and allergic reactions. Fireflies are "poisonous" to birds and lizards that consume them. Being prepared is important. There are physical things you can do, such as wearing appropriate clothing—and know that most entomologists eventually get stung!

banana? This is isopentyl (isoamyl acetate), and its banana smell attracts bees and other Hymenopterans. This is the alarm pheromone that signals others to join in the attack.

Treat the sting. Your body will release histamine, causing itching and swelling in response to a sting. Oral antihistamines, such as Claritin or Zyrtec, block the action of histamine and relieve itching; hydrocortisone cream relieves itching from bites and stings. Some other important guidelines:

- Avoid scratching. It is hard, but resisting will lessen the severity of the sting and you will learn not to scratch.

- Get an adult to help remove the bee's stinger by scraping it out sideways using a credit card or driver's license, to prevent squeezing the venom sack; grasp ticks close to skin with forceps and pull straight out.

- Wash the bite or sting with soap and water.

- Apply a cold compress for at least 10 minutes.

- Raise or elevate the affected area.

- If you have a **severe allergic reaction** such as difficulty breathing (anaphylaxis), it is imperative to use an EpiPen if one is available and *immediately* head for the nearest emergency room.

STING AND BITE CHART

DATE & TIME	STINGING ARTHROPOD	DESCRIPTION OF PAIN	REACTION / DURATION OF PAIN TREATMENT	TREATMENT	YOUR PAIN INDEX NUMBER

Make a chart in your field notebook (see the example above) for stings and bites. Record as much information in it as possible.

- When did this happen?
- What stung you?
- Describe the pain (throbbing, burning, etc.).
- How long did the pain last?
- What treatments did you use?
- Thinking about a time you were stung by a different insect, was this sting worse?

 **SAFETY FIRST!**

Caution: If you have a **severe allergy to stings,** or anaphylaxis:

NEVER collect insects that bite or sting.

ALWAYS carry an EpiPen on collecting outings.

ALWAYS take along a parent, other adult, or responsible friend.

NEVER eat bananas while collecting, or when around wasps or bees, which use a banana smell as a "call to arms," or an alert, to attack a person who smells of banana.

BUG SCIENCE

American entomologist Justin O. Schmidt (born 1947) has developed a **sting pain index.** Look this up on the internet and refer to the scale each time you are stung for unusual descriptions, and make up your own. He described the bullet ant, possibly the worst sting, as "pure, intense, brilliant pain. Like walking over flaming charcoal with a 3-inch [7.5 cm] nail embedded in your heel." (Ouch!) He describes the red paper wasp as, "caustic and burning. Distinctly bitter aftertaste. Like spilling a beaker of hydrochloric acid on a paper cut."

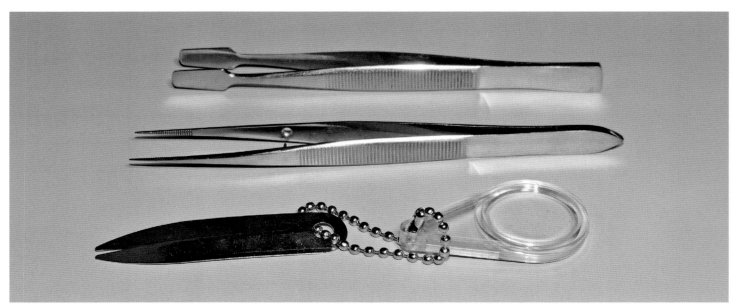

Tick tweezers and forceps

Ticks: Important Arthropod Pests

Ticks are an important arthropod to know because they transmit Lyme disease, Rocky Mountain spotted fever, and other illnesses. They are blood-sucking parasites (an organism dependent on another for its existence) of birds, reptiles, and mammals—including humans—so we need to be as familiar with them as possible to avoid them.

Ticks are a fact of life, and tick behavior is very important to understand to avoid problems with them. Ticks respond to heat, vibrations, and carbon dioxide, all of which we produce as we walk through fields and woods! If you become an "expert" on ticks you can help educate others not familiar with them.

After your next romp through woods and fields, carefully check your pet— and yourself—for ticks.

STEP 1: Put on latex gloves.

STEP 2: Carefully examine your pet. With an adult's help, each time you find a tick, grasp it with forceps as close as possible to your pet's skin and pull it straight out.

STEP 3: Drop the ticks into a lidded jar. Place the top on the jar after each tick is added.

STEP 4: Gently rub each bite site with an alcohol wipe. Do NOT let your pet lick or bite the site.

STEP 5: When finished, pour a little alcohol into the jar, then reseal and tighten the jar top. Dispose of your gloves and wash your hands with soap and water. Wrap the jar in newspaper and dispose with trash headed for the landfill.

STEP 6: Do a very careful tick check of your whole body and take a shower. It is a good idea to ask a parent to assist with the tick check.

SAFETY FIRST!

Caution: If you encounter seed ticks, which are much smaller than other ticks—smaller than a period (".")—and in large numbers, *stop collecting and wipe yourself down thoroughly* (or ask a parent to help) with alcohol wipes.

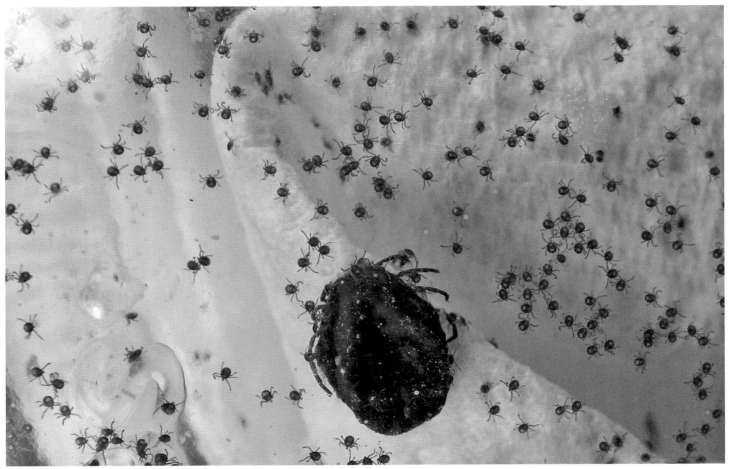

A female tick and a *few* of her larva (offspring)

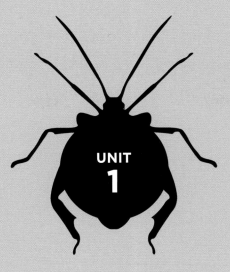

UNIT
1

BEGIN YOUR BUG ADVENTURE

Every great adventure begins with good preparation. This unit equips you with a few essential techniques. We begin by organizing your field notebook and learning a technique for sketching insects. We will consider first aid for bites and stings followed by an experiment with ants. Much can be learned about caring for an arthropod or insect pet.

WHERE TO LOOK

Fig. 1: Logs and fallen trees are great places to look for bugs in the forest.

Bugs are the most common animal on the planet. In fact, our most common interaction with wildlife is with insects. You don't need a collecting kit to get started on the fun—just get out there and look for places to collect bugs. You'll find them virtually everywhere!

MATERIALS

- Insect net
- Your field notebook (see page 12)
- Pencil
- Camera

STEP 1: When in a forest, find a rotting log and step on it as a precaution so that any hiding snakes will slither away. Then roll the log over and watch for roaches and beetles scurrying away (fig. 1). Dig a little into the log and you may find termites and centipedes. Look in thick leaf litter around the bases of trees for millipedes, and in bushes for spiders.

STEP 2: Walk through a field and briskly sweep your net back and forth through the plants on either side and in front of you (fig. 2). You'll find a variety of insects, including some agricultural pests.

STEP 3: Visit a flower or vegetable garden and look for bugs, butterflies, flies, beetles, and spiders (fig. 3).

Fig. 2: When in a field, sweep the plants with a net.

STEP 4: Walk along a stream. Many insects and arthropods live along the bank.

STEP 5: Insects and other arthropods are excellent at camouflage and blend in with the bark on trees, with the grass in fields, and among the leaves in trees (fig. 4).

STEP 6: Keep a record in your field notebook of where you find different insects and other arthropods, and sketch or photograph the ones you find.

Fig. 3: You'll find all kinds of bugs in flower and vegetable gardens.

Fig. 4: Many insects, like this sharpshooter, are masters of camouflage.

BUG SCIENCE

Once you become accustomed to a new environment, you'll be able to find bugs there. An important contribution you can make as a young entomologist is to share cool facts about bugs with your friends and teachers. You'll quickly discover how many people are afraid of bugs. Your ability to find bugs and share your knowledge about them will help others learn to appreciate bugs and realize that most bugs are not bad.

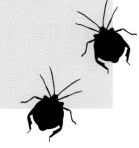

LEARN THROUGH SKETCHING

Examining and sketching insects with a magnifying glass or loupe helps you focus on characteristics used to identify them. There are many kinds of antennae, wing vein patterns, mouthparts, etc. For example, most insects have four wings, but flies have only two. Sketching insects helps you learn their parts.

MATERIALS

- **Insect samples or insect field guide**
- **Loupe or magnifying glass**
- **Paper**
- **Your field notebook**
- **Pencil**

Fig. 1: Use a loupe to sketch an insect's details.

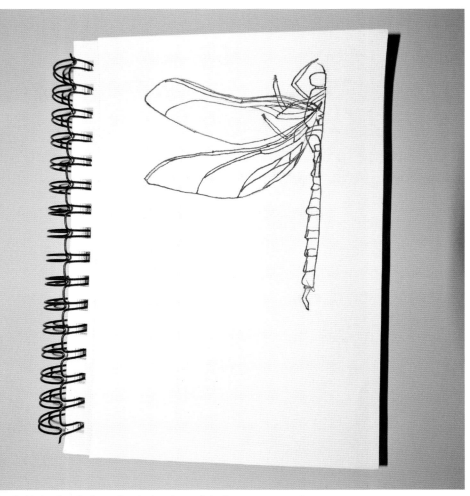

Fig. 2: Make detailed notebook sketches of the insects you study.

BUG SCIENCE

Entomologists use magnifying lenses to examine and identify insects. You can examine bees' pollen "baskets," found on the tibia of their hind legs. They may be bulging with pollen. The structure of antennae is often useful in identifying insects. Termites, for example, have beaded antennae, while ants have antennae that are bent or have an "elbow." Ants are a nuisance and termites can cause a lot of damage to your home, so knowing which you are finding is very important.

STEP 1: Collect an insect or select a picture in a field guide that shows a lot of detail, including legs, antennae, or wings.

STEP 2: Examine your selection, using a loupe to magnify it (fig. 1).

STEP 3: Start with the head and draw what you see through the loupe. Focus on the things you have not noticed or thought about before (fig. 2).

STEP 4: Move to the thorax (middle section) and, finally, the abdomen.

STEP 5: Carefully examine and draw the antennae, legs, and mouthparts. These can be separate sketches.

The "scientific method" is a systematic procedure scientists use to answer a question or solve a problem—here, ants getting into the house.

Experimenting with Ants

Using the scientific method, we can learn about the meaning of ants' trails. Ants communicate with each other by using chemicals called *pheromones*. When they find food, they leave a pheromone trail so other ants can find their way to the food, too. In this experiment, we will try to find something that will disrupt this trail.

MATERIALS

- Trail disrupters (kitchen spices, baby powder, petroleum jelly, etc.)
- Your field notebook
- Pencil
- Small jar
- Rubbing alcohol (isopropyl alcohol 60%)
- Loupe or magnifying glass

STEP 1: Identify and define your insect problem. Ants are getting into the house and we need to block their path.

STEP 2: Do a literature review for things that may interrupt ants' trails, such as black pepper or cayenne pepper, and other things—baby powder, petroleum jelly.

STEP 3: Design your experiment. Make a data table in your field notebook as shown at right. Title the page "Ant Trail Experiment." List everything you will try as a barrier to the ants.

STEP 4: Find an ant trail and spread a line of material, one material at a time, across the ants' trail. Wait to see if they cross it or go around. Record your observations. Then try each of the other materials one at a time, recording your results in the table.

STEP 5: Collect a few ants with which you have been experimenting and put them into a jar with a small amount of rubbing alcohol to kill them. Select an ant, remove it from the jar, and let it dry before taping it to the page in your field

ANT TRAIL EXPERIMENT

DATE & LOCATION	TRIAL	SPICE OR BARRIER	REACTION OF ANTS	SUCCESS OF BARRIER
	1			
	2			
	3			

notebook where you report the results of your experiment. Using your loupe to magnify the ant, draw a picture in your field notebook, and add details of the activity you observed (fig. 1).

There are hundreds of different kinds of ants. It may be difficult, but try to find the name of the ant species you collected. "Families" are groups of related species. You may find the "family" of the species you collected, if you cannot find the species. Most states have an Extension Service with an ant specialist who can assist in identifying your ant. You may find this specialist by searching the internet using your state name followed by "extension service entomologist."

Often, experiments are not successful on the first try, so we redesign them and repeat them. Even when they are not successful we learn things. You will probably need to repeat this experiment several times, searching for something that will interrupt an ant's trail.

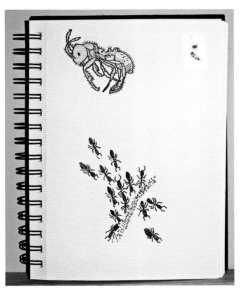

Fig. 1: An "Ant Trail Experiment" field notebook page with an ant taped to it.

BUG SCIENCE

One of the best-known entomologists, E. O. Wilson (born 1929), specialized in ants. He described using ant trail pheromones to lead ants to food. To replicate his experiment, place a just-killed grasshopper, cricket, or moth in the corner of a sheet of posterboard. Then place another freshly killed grass-hopper, cricket, or moth at the opposite corner. Use forceps to collect ants as needed near the first dead insect. Squeeze each ant's abdomen to collect the liquid (pheromones) expelled onto a pointed skewer. Use the skewer to draw a line of pheromones from the second insect to the first. Time and record how long it takes ants to find the second insect. Make your comparisons.

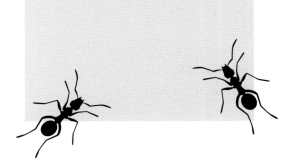

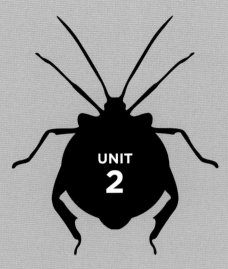

UNIT 2

MAKE & USE A COLLECTING KIT

In studying insects and other arthropods, entomologists need equipment, and most is relatively easy to construct. A net is possibly the most important tool for collecting insects. A thorough study of insects requires live and dead specimens, so critter keepers and kill jars are very important. These labs include making and learning to use an insect net and collecting jars.

MAKE AN INSECT NET

MATERIALS

- Scissors
- 1 piece of mosquito netting or muslin slightly larger than 45 inches × 24 inches (114 × 61 cm)
- Sewing machine, or needle and thread
- Straight pins
- 45-inch × 8-inch (114 × 20 cm) square piece of sailcloth or denim
- 4 feet (120 cm) of heavy (#8) steel wire
- 5-gallon (19-l) plastic bucket
- 1 (2- to 4-foot-long, or 60 to 120 cm) broomstick or wooden dowel (whatever length works best for you)
- Pocketknife
- Drill
- 3-inch (8-cm) long aluminum or PVC pipe (optional)
- Screwdriver (optional)
- Screw (optional)
- Permanent marker

A net is the most important tool used by entomologists—and they're fun to make. You will need an adult to help you with this project.

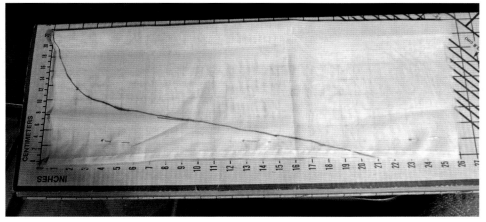

Fig. 1: Fold the muslin over, and draw a line as shown.

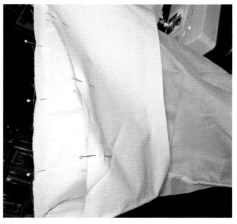

Fig. 2: Pin the casing around the top of the net.

STEP 1: Fold the netting in half and draw a line as shown (fig. 1). Cut along the curved line and then sew the cut edges together. This will form a bag.

STEP 2: Fold over a piece of sailcloth or denim and pin it around the top of the bag, reinforcing the top of the net and forming a tunnel, or casing, through which the metal loop will be threaded (figs. 2 and 3).

STEP 3: Bend the steel wire into a circle around the plastic bucket to get a smooth bend. Then bend both ends away from the circle (fig. 4). These will attach to the handle. One side should be 2¾ inches (7 cm) long and the other, 3¾ inches (9.5 cm) long.

(continued)

Fig. 3: Fold the casing over.

Fig. 4: Bend the wire around the bucket, and bend the ends away from the circle.

STEP 4: Bend ¼ inch (6 mm) of the ends in toward each other. With your pocketknife, carefully carve a 2½-inch (6.5 cm) groove and a 3½-inch (9 cm) groove on opposite sides of one end of the broomstick or dowel. Drill a small hole into the handle at the inside end of each groove for the wire ends to fit into (fig. 5). The wire will lay into the grooves and the ends will bend into the handle.

STEP 5: Thread the wire into the sailcloth tunnel (fig. 6). Seat the wire ends in their corresponding grooves and tuck the ends into the holes (fig. 7). If you like, slide a short piece of pipe up the handle and over the ends of the wire and secure it with a screw into the net handle on the opposite side of the tubing from the net.

STEP 6: Write your name and phone number on your net.

STEP 7: Now it is time to chase bugs (fig. 8)!

Fig. 5: The tips of the wire ends bend in; carefully make the grooves and holes in the handle.

BUG SCIENCE

You will become very attached to your net and will carry it with you on all trips—whether you intend to collect or not. You will enjoy having it just to catch, identify, or examine and release. It gives you a longer reach and good exercise. It will become an extension of your arm and will protect you from having to handle insects that may be dangerous.

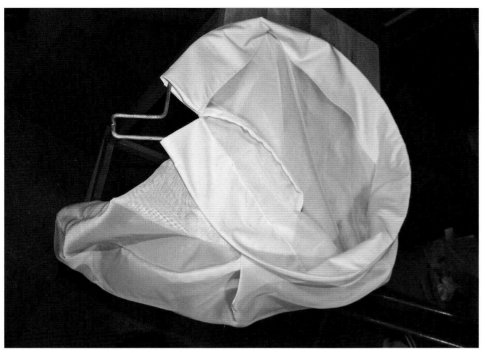

Fig. 6: Thread the wire through the casing.

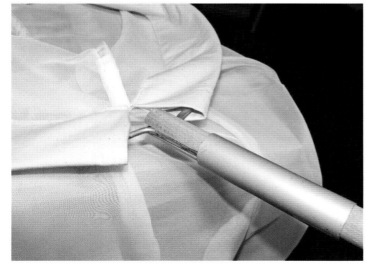

Fig. 7: Seat the wire into the handle's grooves and tuck the ends into the holes. Secure the pipe to the handle, if desired.

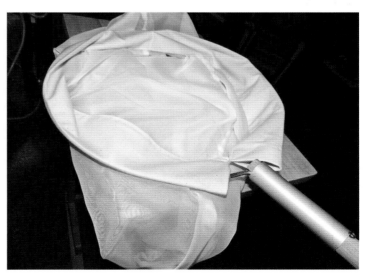

Fig. 8: Finished net—let's go chase bugs!

HOW TO USE AN INSECT NET

Take your insect net into the field to collect your specimens. Knowing a little about insect behavior will help you become skillful with your net. Many insects fly or crawl "up" to avoid predators. Follow the directions here to become an expert net user.

MATERIALS

- **Your insect net (see Lab 4, page 28)**
- **Collection jar (optional; see Lab 7, page 36)**
- **Your field notebook**
- **Pencil**

STEP 1: Flying insects are most easily collected by swinging the net "up" and from "behind" the insect. Insect nets are not fly swatters!

STEP 2: Once an insect is inside the net, twist or rotate the handle to block, or close, its opening (fig. 1). As you do this, watch and keep twisting the net in the same direction to keep the insect climbing "up" and toward the end of the net.

STEP 3: When it reaches the end of the net, grasp the net just below the insect.

STEP 4: You can now examine it or put it in the appropriate collection jar, if you like.

STEP 5: Record your collection results in your field notebook, along with the date and location.

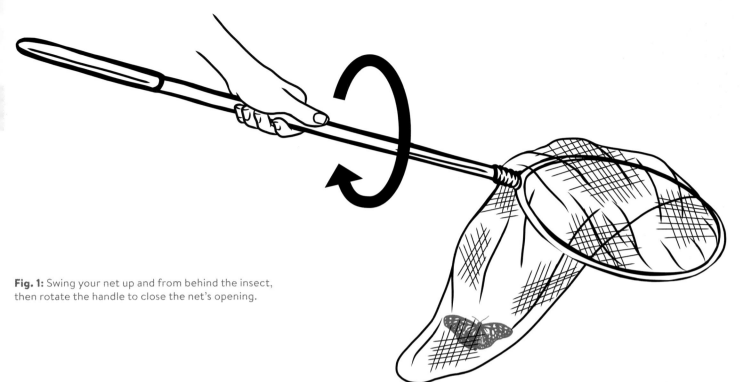

Fig. 1: Swing your net up and from behind the insect, then rotate the handle to close the net's opening.

BUG SCIENCE

An insect's typical escape response is to fly or climb up. Knowing this will help improve your collecting strategy and success. After collecting an insect, twist the handle to close the opening. Continue twisting the handle in the same direction so the insect will crawl to the end of the net. At this point, gather the insect by securing it in the end of the net, allowing the rest to unfold. Remove the lid of the dry jar and slide it into the net. Pull the end of the net down around the jar, forcing the insect into the jar. With the net still against the jar, turn the jar upside down. The insect will crawl toward the bottom of the jar past the paper towel. With your other hand, reach into the net and put the lid on the still upside-down jar. Use the same technique with the wet jar, but instead of turning the jar over, thump the insect clinging to the net so it falls into the alcohol and quickly dies. Remove the net and put the lid on the jar.

CARING FOR ARTHROPODS

Hercules beetle larva.

Arthropods are invertebrates (animals with no spinal column) that have segmented bodies and a hard outer shell. Arthropods include insects, spiders, scorpions, millipedes, crayfish, and ticks. They make up more than 90 percent of all living animals! Learning to care for arthropods for a few days can be educational and enjoyable.

MATERIALS

- **Your insect net (see Lab 4, page 28)**
- **Trowel**
- **Critter keeper or small glass jar (such as a peanut butter jar with small holes made in the lid)**
- **Small bowl, bottle cap, or a piece of a sponge for water**
- **Thin plastic sheet or plastic wrap**
- **Hole punch or other sharp tool (use caution!)**
- **Your field notebook**
- **Pencil**

STEP 1: Collect arthropods in a net, jar, or critter keeper (fig. 1).

STEP 2: Collect some of the soil and pieces of decaying wood or samples of the plant they are living on from the location where you collected the arthropod. Plant-eating insects will need a steady supply of plants to sustain them (figs. 2 and 3).

STEP 3: Identify the arthropod and search for its name followed by "care sheet" on the internet. This will provide more specific suggestions for food or host plants and care.

STEP 4: Provide water and food (fig. 4). Slices of apple or carrot, lettuce, dry dog food, and crickets are common foods used with various arthropods, but different ones have different needs.

STEP 5: Punch a few holes in a piece of thin plastic or plastic wrap. Stretch it over the critter keeper, beneath its top, to help maintain the necessary moisture level.

STEP 6: Monitor your arthropod's health. In most cases, you should release it within a few hours or a few days at the longest.

STEP 7: Keep a record in your field notebook of your care for your arthropod.

STEP 8: Release it where you found it.

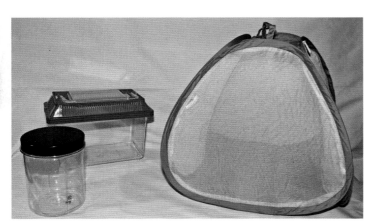

Fig. 1: Critter keepers are useful for keeping arthropods for a few days.

Figs. 2 and 3: A fishing spider (left) and beetles in their habitats.

BUG SCIENCE

Keeping live arthropods is an important responsibility—you will need to check on them every day. You will need to provide food, water, shelter, and space. Critter keepers (commonly available at pet stores and big box stores) are useful for keeping arthropods for a few days. Looking closely at the habitat where you collected the arthropod will provide powerful clues as to what they need in captivity. If they were eating leaves, collect some for them. If they are living under or in a log, collect some of the log as well. If the log is in the forest and moist, keep the log moist in your critter keeper.

Fig. 4: Provide adequate water for your arthropod. Is it a millipede like this one?

Collections are essential in entomology. Collecting jars enables you to collect high-quality specimens, killing them quickly to prevent them from damaging delicate wings and other parts, and allowing you to collect multiple insects in the same jar.

In this lab, we make one of each type of standard kill jar: "wet" and "dry." A relaxing jar (see Lab 15, page 62) is useful, too, when you do not have time to empty and pin insects from the killing jars.

MATERIALS

TO MAKE A WET JAR

- Duct tape (optional)
- 1 wide-mouth half-pint (240 ml) glass jar with a lid
- 1 bottle rubbing alcohol (isopropyl alcohol, 60%)
- Label
- Permanent marker

TO USE A WET JAR

- 1 wet collecting jar
- Your insect net (see Lab 4, page 28)

Important: ALWAYS clearly label your collecting jars immediately after you make them.

Fig. 1: A wet jar in use.

BUG SCIENCE

Use the **wet jar** for aphids, ants, bees, centipedes, fleas, lice, mayflies, millipedes, pill bugs, scales, scorpions, silverfish, spiders, springtails, stoneflies, termites, thrips, ticks, and wasps. Alcohol kills them very quickly. Many insects can be placed in the wet jar together.

Ants, bees, and wasps can be put in either a wet jar or a dry jar (see page 38). They die more quickly in the wet jar's alcohol, and you eliminate the risk they will damage other specimens in the dry jar.

MAKING AND USING A WET JAR

STEP 1: If desired, wrap a couple layers of duct tape around the bottom of the jar to protect it from breaking and to make it easier to clean up if it does break.

STEP 2: Place about 2 inches (5 cm) of rubbing alcohol in the half-pint (240 ml) jar. Periodically, you will need to add more. Immediately label the jar with a skull and crossbones and/or the word "Poison." Secure the lid.

STEP 3: When you have an insect in the end of your net, remove the wet jar's lid and keep the jar right-side up as you work the net down and around the jar. When you get the net tight across the top, the insect will most often cling to the net above the alcohol. A thump on the net stretched tight over the top of the wet jar will send it tumbling into the alcohol, where it will die very fast (fig. 1). Secure the lid.

Be careful to keep leaves, grass, and other plant material out of the wet jar because chlorophyll will leach out, giving the alcohol a green color.

SAFETY FIRST!

NEVER leave a kill jar open. Add or remove insects, then close the jar.

Label all kill jars with a skull and crossbones symbol, and, if you like, the word POISON. **This step is very important. Do NOT skip it.**

MATERIALS

TO MAKE A DRY JAR

- Duct tape (optional)
- 1 wide-mouth pint (480 ml) glass jar with a lid
- Sawdust
- Pencil
- 1 sheet of paper
- Scissors
- Flat-bottomed stick (the larger the better)
- Plaster of Paris
- 1 bottle non-acetone nail polish remover (ethyl acetate)
- Paper towel
- Label
- Permanent marker

TO USE A DRY JAR

- Your insect net (see Lab 4, page 28)
- 1 dry collecting jar

MAKING AND USING A DRY JAR

STEP 1: If desired, wrap a couple layers of duct tape around the bottom of the jar to protect it from breaking and to make it easier to clean up if it does break.

STEP 2: Place about 2 inches (5 cm) of sawdust in the bottom of a pint (480 ml) jar (fig. 1).

STEP 3: Place the jar on your piece of paper and trace a circle around the bottom. Cut out the circle, slightly smaller than what you traced, and place it on top of the sawdust. Tamp down the sawdust with your stick (fig. 2) to about 1 inch (2.5 cm).

STEP 4: Follow the manufacturer's directions to mix the plaster of Paris with water, or add water until the plaster of Paris is pourable. Pour in enough plaster of Paris, on top of the paper, to cover by about 1 inch (2.5 cm). Let it dry. This may take several days. Leave the top off the jar until the plaster is dry. Air conditioners cool and dry air, so placing a jar in front of an air conditioner or in an air-conditioned room will speed drying, if possible.

STEP 5: Once the plaster dries, pour just enough non-acetone nail polish remover into the jar as will soak into the plaster of Paris. If it soaks in very quickly, add a little more. You do not want liquid standing in the jar, so pour any excess into another jar to use later.

STEP 6: Loosely wad up a piece of paper towel and drop it into the jar.

The paper towel prevents butterflies and moths from flapping their wings and knocking the scales off. Immediately label the jar with a skull and crossbones and/or the word "Poison." Secure the lid.

STEP 7: You will need to recharge your dry jar with non-acetone nail polish remover every day, or every day you use it.

STEP 8: When you have an insect in the end of your net, give the net a twist, remove the dry jar's lid and slide the jar into the net, holding the net secure around the jar. When the butterfly or other insect is at the mouth of the open jar, turn the jar bottom up holding the net secure around the jar. The insect

BUG SCIENCE

Butterflies and moths should always be placed in a **dry jar**, because alcohol will dislodge their scales. The dry jar can be used for other insects as well, but they should be collected separately from butterflies or moths to keep them from destroying their wings.

Fig. 1: Place the sawdust layer in the jar.

Fig. 2: Place the paper circle in the jar and tamp down the sawdust. Then add a layer of plaster of Paris, let dry completely, and charge the plaster with non-acetone nail polish remover. Cover tightly and label clearly as poison.

Fig. 3: Dry jar in use. Paper towel helps keep the insect from flapping its wings and knocking off its scales.

will begin working its way "up" toward the bottom of the jar past the paper towel (fig. 3). An insect's nature is to escape by flying or climbing up. Working its way between the paper towel and side of the jar prevents moths and butterflies from flapping their wings and knocking off their scales. If you turn the jar with the opening facing up, the insect will change direction and head for the opening; secure the lid on the jar while it is upside down and then remove it from the net.

ANOTHER COLLECTING METHOD

In addition to collecting jars, you can freeze insects in a plastic bag to kill them. However, some cold-resistant insects will need to be frozen for two or three days and in separate bags.

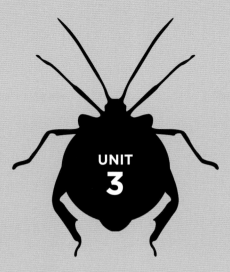

ADVANCED COLLECTING TECHNIQUES

This unit describes advanced techniques used to collect insects, taking advantage of what we know about small insects, insects that are well camouflaged in bushes, nocturnal insects, and ground insects. Practicing these skills is enjoyable and will increase the diversity of insects in your collection.

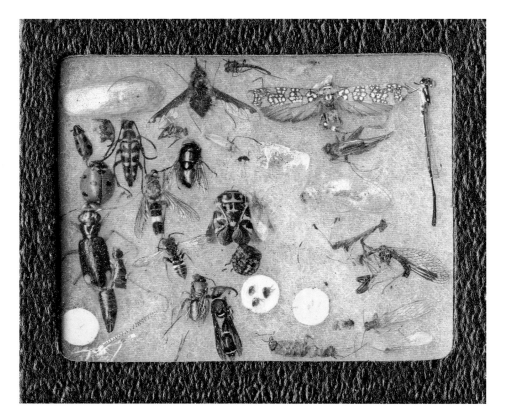

MATERIALS

- Ice pick, nail, leather hole punch, or drill with a bit smaller than the tubing (use caution!)
- Clean pill bottle with cap
- 1-inch (2.5 cm) diameter small circular piece of gauze or other mesh
- 1 (18-inch, or 46 cm) piece of small plastic aquarium tubing
- 1 (6-inch, or 15 cm) piece of small plastic aquarium tubing
- Your field notebook
- Pencil
- Loupe or magnifying glass

STEP 1: Assemble your materials (fig. 1). With the help of an adult, punch or drill two holes in the pill bottle cap small enough that the tubing is difficult to insert and not easily removed.

STEP 2: Place your gauze over the end of the 18-inch (46-cm) piece of tubing. Push the tubing, gauze-end first, about ½ inch to ¾ inch (1 to 2 cm) into one of the holes in the cap (fig. 2). You will use this tube to suck insects into the vial and the gauze will prevent you from accidentally inhaling an arthropod or two.

The greatest diversity in insects is in the very small ones. The quickest way to make a great collection is to collect small insects. Many insects are too small to collect with a net, so an aspirator, or "pooter" (see page 43), with which they can safely be sucked into a bottle is used.

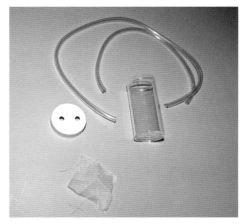

Fig. 1: Materials for making a pooter.

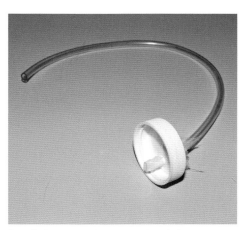

Fig. 2: First tube (your mouth tube) with gauze covering the end, inserted into cap.

STEP 3: Push about the same amount (½ inch to ¾ inch, or 1 to 2 cm) of the end of the second tube through the cap (fig. 3). This tube will be used to suck insects into the aspirator. The gauze on the bottom of the other tube will prevent you from eating them.

STEP 4: Put the cap on the bottle (fig. 4). Collect some small insects by sucking on the large tube while holding the short tube near the insect. Place the insects into a kill jar, or freeze them in a sealable plastic bag or jar. Keep your pooter dry at all times.

STEP 5: Record in your field notebook what you collected. Use a loupe to magnify them so you can sketch pictures in your field notebook.

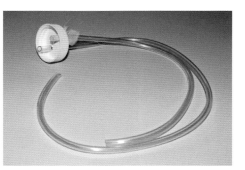

Fig. 3: Second tube (for sucking insects into the aspirator) inserted into cap.

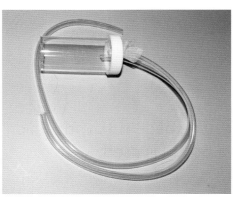

Fig. 4: Your finished aspirator.

BUG SCIENCE

Arthropods, such as thrips or mites, are very easy to collect with an aspirator, or "pooter," so called in honor of American entomologist F. William Poos, Jr. (1891–1987), who published an aspirator design in 1929. These bugs are a little more difficult to identify, but they make an incredible "shirt pocket" collection! The collection pictured on the opposite page is 2½ inches × 2½ inches (6 × 6 cm) and features more than twenty orders.

SAFETY FIRST!

Caution: Formic acid is an irritating chemical in the sprayed venom of some ant species. Sucking a few—fewer than five ants—is not harmful. However, if you feel a dryness or burning in your throat, *stop collecting.*

USE A BEAT STICK & BEAT SHEET

A quick way to make an assessment or a collection of the bugs in a bush or tree is to use a beat stick to strike its branches to dislodge them, and to catch them in a beat sheet underneath it. Do not beat the bush hard enough to damage it!

MATERIALS

- One 3-foot (1 m) square white cloth
- 1 yardstick (meter stick)—your beat stick
- Camera (optional)
- 1 wet collecting jar (see Lab 7, page 36)
- 1 dry collecting jar (see Lab 7, page 38)
- Forceps or tweezers
- Your field notebook
- Pencil

STEP 1: Spread the white cloth under a bush to act as a beat sheet. You can place something heavy, like a rock, on each corner to help keep it in place. Use your beat stick (fig. 1) to strike the limbs of the bush, dislodging insects onto the beat sheet where they can be collected or photographed, if you like (fig. 2).

STEP 2: The insects from each bush should be placed into the appropriate collecting jar (see Lab 7, page 36 for review). Use forceps or tweezers to handle the insects.

STEP 3: After identifying the insects and number of orders represented, list them in your field notebook.

BUG SCIENCE

Insects are masters of camouflage and mimicry. It is surprising how many can be hiding in plain sight in a bush or on small tree limbs.

Fig. 1: Beat sheet and beat stick.

Fig. 2: Small insects on your beat sheet dislodged from the bush with your beat stick.

MAKE & USE A PITFALL TRAP

Fig. 4: The cover helps keep rain from flooding your trap.

MATERIALS

- Four 2-inch (5 cm) wood blocks
- 1-inch (2.5 cm) thick wood board or ⅛-inch (3 mm) thick plywood, 12 inches (30.5 cm) square
- Four 3-inch (8 cm) Phillips flat-head screws and screwdriver (if using a board) *or* wood glue (if using plywood)
- Trowel or spade
- Bulb planter (optional)
- 16-ounce (474 ml) plastic cup
- 4 to 6 ounces (119 to 178 ml) water
- Dishwashing liquid

Insects, spiders, and other arthropods continually crawl around forests and grasslands. You can use pitfall traps to collect them—and you don't need to be there while they're working around the clock!

SAFETY FIRST!

You'll need adult supervision and help if you use screws to assemble your trap cover.

STEP 1: Make a cover for your trap by attaching a block to each corner of a board with screws, or gluing them in place on plywood (figs. 1 and 2).

STEP 2: Use a trowel or spade to dig a hole the same diameter and depth as the disposable cup. (A bulb planter may also be helpful for this task.) Place the cup in the ground so its lip is at ground level (fig. 3).

STEP 3: Pour the water into the cup. Add a few drops of dishwashing liquid. The soap will break the surface tension of the water so the arthropods that fall into it will drown quickly.

STEP 4: Place the cover over the trap to keep rain from filling the cup (fig. 4). Some entomologists position sticks to guide insects into their traps.

STEP 5: Check every day or two and remove the arthropods. You'll be amazed to find how many insects, spiders, and other arthropods you'll catch.

STEP 6: Lightly rinse the insects. Let dry before pinning and adding to your collection (see Lab 15, page 62).

Fig. 1: Attach the wood blocks to the wood board with screws, or glue them to plywood.

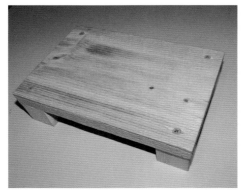

Fig. 2: The completed cover.

Fig. 3: Dig a hole the same diameter and depth as the cup.

LAB 11 BLACKLIGHTING

Searching for insects at night is fun, too! Using black lights at night to attract insects to sheets hanging between trees is a popular collecting method.

MATERIALS

- About 8 feet (240 cm) of rope
- 5 large binder clips, plus more as needed
- 2 old, light-colored bed sheets
- 2 tent stakes or bricks
- Black light (12-volt or 110-volt)
- Access to electricity with 120-volt lights or a 12-volt battery for battery-powered black lights
- 1 wet collection jar (see Lab 7, page 36)
- 1 dry collection jar (see Lab 7, page 38)

STEP 1: Tie a rope between two trees in your yard or a nearby park, or suspend it from supports on a porch. It should be suspended at about the young entomologist's height.

STEP 2: Use binder clips to hang one bed sheet from the rope. Place the second sheet on the ground under the hanging sheet.

STEP 3: Use tent stakes or bricks to secure the bottom corners of the hanging sheet to the ground.

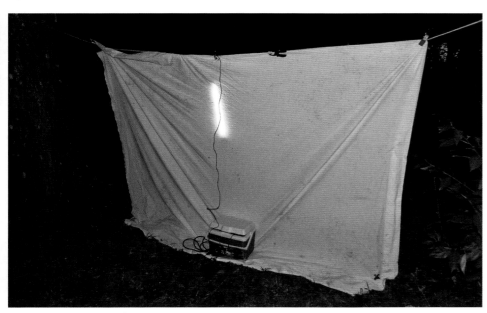

Fig. 1: Setting up a black light.

BUG SCIENCE

It is amazing how many insects are active at night. All collectors have stories about large moths they have collected! There are probably fourteen moths to every butterfly, and moths are active at night. Expect to collect many more moths at night than butterflies during the day (fig. 2). And lots of beetles and other insects are also attracted to the black light.

Blacklighting is always better during the new moon phase because moths use the moon for navigation, which is not so visible during new moon. This could become your favorite collecting technique!

STEP 4: Hang a black light over the sheet and secure its power cord at the top with a binder clip.

STEP 5: Connect the light to an outlet or battery for power. At dusk, turn on the light (figs. 1 and 2).

STEP 6: Use your wet and dry jars to collect insects. However, collecting off a sheet is different. Both jars are held upright and their lids are used to "eat" the insects off the sheet like Pac-Man. Using the dry jar, bring the jar up beneath the moth on the sheet while bringing the lid down from above to trap it into the jar.

STEP 7: Different insects come out at different times of night. Moths, beetles, bugs, and others come out at night. Sometimes larger moths come out later.

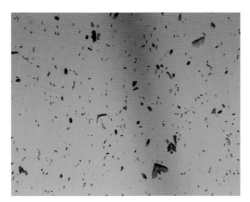

Fig. 2: The black light attracts bugs to the sheet.

UNIT
4

PRESERVING INSECTS

Preserving insects is very important, because it records their history. For instance, notable drops in bumblebee populations over the past fifty years in England and the northeastern United States have been discovered to be related to the change in land use.

PHOTOGRAPHING INSECTS

A young entomologist learning to position and photograph insects.

MATERIALS

- **Camera**
- **Critter keeper (optional)**
- **White bowl (optional)**
- **Petroleum jelly if you use the bowl**
- **Your field notebook**
- **Pencil**
- **Laptop or computer (optional)**

There are so many excellent digital cameras and smartphone cameras today that the nature of studying insects and insect collections themselves are changing. Practice a lot with your camera to understand how it works—you'll never miss a great shot again!

STEP 1: Insects and arthropods are small, so you will need to be as close as possible to take their picture, but not so close that you scare them away. Practice enlarging the image area on your camera for the perfect distance (fig. 1). Clip-on magnifiers for digital cameras are also excellent for photographing small insects and other arthropods.

STEP 2: If you're not in the "wild," critter keepers with open tops are great. Put some twigs or leaves from the bush it was on into the critter keeper, place the insect on top, and photograph it through the open critter keeper top (fig. 2).

STEP 3: Focusing on the antennae or legs will help you get better-focused photos.

Fig. 1: Practice enlarging the image area when photographing insects with your phone's camera.

Fig. 2: Experiment with different backgrounds for your insects.

BUG SCIENCE

A collection of photographs is not nearly as useful as preserved specimens; however, they are very useful in a "bioblitz," where you document the specimens in an area over a 24-hour period, or when you do not have your collecting equipment with you. Most entomologists arrange their photos by order (Coleoptera, Hymenoptera, Lepidoptera, etc.) on their computers, along with the information that would be on locator labels, such as genus, species, date collected, location or geographic coordinates, and the name of the photographer.

STEP 4: Expect to take at least six to eight photos to get one good photo (fig. 3). Delete the ones that are out of focus to save space on your memory card.

STEP 5: You can chill insects to slow them down by putting them in the refrigerator for 15 to 20 minutes first. You need to be ready to photograph them when you take them out because they warm up and become active quickly!

STEP 6: A large white bowl makes a good place to put insects and other arthropods for photographing them. Spread some petroleum jelly around the top inch (2.5 cm) of the bowl to help prevent them from crawling out.

STEP 7: Keep a record in your field notebook of when and where each photo was taken and what the arthropod was doing, as well as the name of the plant it was on, if you know it. Cameras save the date on photos, and some even record the location You can

Fig. 3: Photographing insects in their natural setting.

even try photographing them at night! Do you notice any differences?

STEP 8: Organize your insect photos on your computer by insect order.

LAB 13

SPIDERWEB PHOTO HUNT

Spiders use their silk in many ways: to alert them when something has touched their web, to catch and secure prey, to communicate with or attract a mate, to mark their territory, to catch the wind and take them to a new location, as a drag line to support their weight, and more!

Fig. 1: An orb web.

Fig. 2: A golden silk orb-weaver and web.

MATERIALS
- **Your field notebook**
- **Pencil**
- **Camera**

STEP 1: Review the photos of different web patterns. Some spiders have incredibly complex webs, and different spiders make different types.

• The golden silk orb-weaver weaves an "orb" web with golden silk (figs. 1 and 2), possibly to attract bees.

• The spiny orb-weaver's web is supported by lines of silk that have thick and thin areas (fig. 3)! The thick-and-thin strands are visible to birds and mammals (including humans) to prevent them from flying or walking through their webs and damaging them.

• The web of the black and yellow garden spider also includes a distinctive element called a *stabilimentum*, or web decoration (fig. 4).

Also be on the lookout for funnel webs, bowl and doily webs, and sheet webs (figs. 5–7), as well as others, such as spiral orb webs, dome webs, tangle webs, and cobwebs. You're sure to find them in unexpected places (fig. 8).

(continued)

Fig. 3: A spiny orb-weaver and web.

Fig. 4: A black and yellow garden spider and web with stabilimentum.

Fig. 6: Bowl and doily webs.

Fig. 7: A sheet web.

BUG SCIENCE

Spiders are possibly the most abundant and neglected arthropods on the planet! More than 200 different species have been collected on a wildlife refuge near the author's home. There's much to learn about and enjoy while looking for and photographing spiders' incredibly complex and varied webs.

Spiders suffer from an undeserved bad reputation. The vast majority aren't dangerous, but you should get to know the ones in your area that are. It's fine to sketch and photograph the spiders and webs you observe, but don't touch or handle them! (See Safety First, page 57.)

Fig. 5: A funnel web.

Fig. 8: A web woven over a pitcher plant.

SPIDERWEB OBSERVATIONS

WEB TYPE	LOCATION	SPIDER (IF SEEN)	STICKY?	NUMBER OBSERVED	OBSERVATIONS
ORB					
FUNNEL					
SHEET					

STEP 2: Create a chart in your field notebook like the one shown above to keep a record of how many of each type of web you find. What do you think will be the most common?

STEP 3: Sketch a picture of and photograph each web you see. Touch it to see if it's sticky but be careful to not destroy it. Did you see the spider? Did it respond to you touching its web? If you get a photo of the spider you may be able to identify it.

STEP 4: When in the woods or field, be on the lookout for a leaf, pine needle, or pebble suspended by a thin strand of silk and twisting in the air. Follow the strand up into the trees until you can see the web it's helping to keep stretched open.

STEP 5: If you're visiting a place where you've seen a lot of webs, purchase a dozen crickets and place one into each web to observe the spiders' reactions.

STEP 6: Record all your observations in your field notebook.

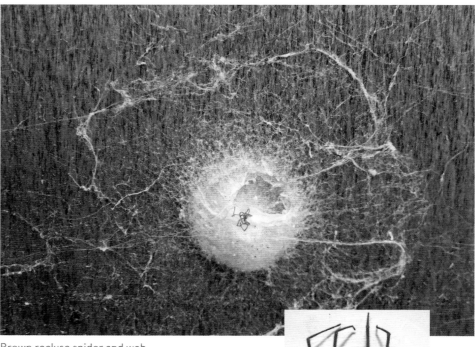

Brown recluse spider and web

Black widow spider in its web

Yellow sac spider

Brazilian wandering spider

SAFETY FIRST!

DO NOT collect or handle spiders. Every region has venomous spiders, including brown recluse and black and brown widows in the United States; redback and funnel-web spiders in Australia, New Zealand, and Southeast Asia; Brazilian wandering and Chilean recluse spiders in South America; six-eyed sand spiders in Africa; and various species of the yellow sac spider in many countries. **Enjoy spiders, but don't touch or kill them!**

MAKE A SPREADING BOARD

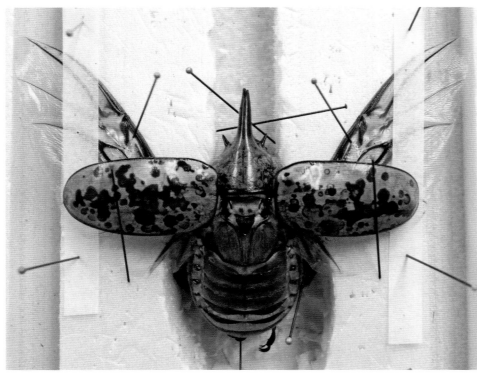

An example of a pinned insect. Here, a Hercules beetle.

Spreading boards, which have a groove that supports the insect's body, are used to pin insects in the best position for drying so that their key features are clearly visible. For example, if a butterfly's wings are not spread, they will dry closed, which will prevent its proper identification.

It is best to become skilled at pinning moths and butterflies before attempting more complicated insects, such as this Hercules beetle. Its hard forewings cover delicate hidden hind wings that are easy to damage if you haven't had lots of practice.

MATERIALS

TO MAKE A CARDBOARD OR CORKBOARD BOARD

- **Corrugated cardboard or corkboard**
- **Craft knife**
- **Ruler**
- **Quilting pins**

FOR STORAGE (SEE PAGE 65)

- **1 storage box or insect collection box (about 19 inches × 16 inches, or 48 × 41 cm), or a shallow cardboard box**
- **1 mothball**

MAKING A CARDBOARD OR CORKBOARD BOARD

STEP 1: Cut three pieces of cardboard or corkboard each 6 inches (15 cm) wide and 16 inches (41 cm) long.

STEP 2: Cut four pieces that are each 2½ inches (6 cm) wide and 10 inches (25 cm) long.

STEP 3: Stack the three larger pieces. You want enough thickness for the length of the pins to penetrate and so channels can be cut in the board to cradle insects' bodies. Position two stacks of two narrower pieces on top of the larger pieces, with enough space between them for the body of the butterfly or moth you want to mount (about ¼ inch, or 6 mm). Secure the cardboard pieces with quilting pins, sticking them straight down through the layers (fig. 1).

Fig. 1: A cork spreading board

Fig. 1: Use the straight edge of your ruler to guide your cuts.

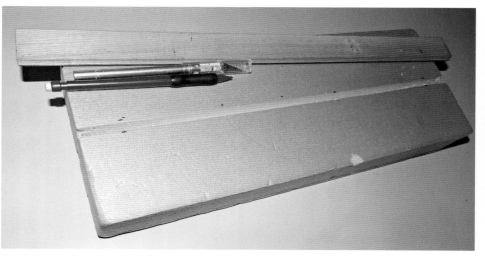

Fig. 2: Finished groove in the foam board supports the insects' bodies

MATERIALS

TO MAKE A FOAM SPREADING BOARD

• **Foam insulation board or foam from an old ice chest (flat and at least 2 inches, or 5 cm, thick); 18 inches × 6 inches (46 × 15 cm) is a good size**

• **Craft knife**

• **Ruler**

FOR STORAGE

• **1 storage box or insect collection box (about 19 inches × 16 inches, or 48 × 41 cm), or a shallow cardboard box**

• **1 mothball**

MAKING A FOAM SPREADING BOARD

STEP 1: Cut pieces of insulating foam (as many as you need for your collection) into strips each about 16 inches (41 cm) long and 6 inches (15 cm) wide.

STEP 2: Using the straight edge of your ruler to guide your cuts, carefully cut a V-shaped groove lengthwise in the center of your board pieces, about ¼ inch (6 mm) wide at the top and tapering to a point about ⅜ inch (9 mm) deep (figs. 1 and 2). This groove will accommodate the body of butterflies so their wings can be secured flat on the spreading board. See example on page 58. Larger grooves may be required for larger butterfly bodies.

STEP 3: For information on storing your collection, see page 65.

BUG SCIENCE

Insects are moved from spreading boards to a collection box after they are dry. This could take several days, depending on the insect and humidity. If a moth or butterfly's wings droop a few days after you move it to a collection, it was removed from the spreading boards too quickly.

Insects are arranged in collections by order, which are arranged alphabetically. As your skills improve, you will enjoy learning the families within each order and arranging the insects accordingly.

A young entomologist displaying his insects on a foam board

LAB
15

HOW TO PIN INSECTS

Fig. 1: A young entomologist carefully pinning insects

Properly spreading and pinning your insects helps you study them. A moth or butterfly that is not spread will have folded wings that, when dry, are impossible to study without breaking. Properly pinned and spread, they are easy to study and beautiful to look at.

MATERIALS

TO MAKE A RELAXING JAR

- Small sponge, cut to fit the bottom of your jar
- Lysol
- 1 wide-mouth pint (475 ml) glass or plastic jar
- Cardboard
- Scissors

FOR PINNING

- Insects
- Insect pins
- Spreading board (see Lab 14, page 58)
- Scissors
- Tracing paper
- Index cards

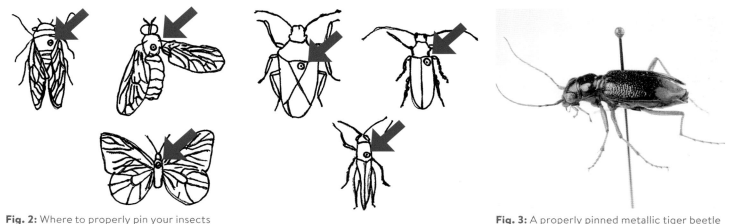

Fig. 2: Where to properly pin your insects

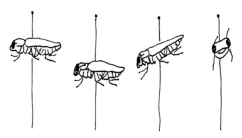

Fig. 3: A properly pinned metallic tiger beetle

STEP 1: As soon as an insect is dead, pin it (fig. 1). If you wait too long, it will become brittle and break as you work with it. You can make a relaxing jar for dry insects that are not brittle.

MAKING A RELAXING JAR

STEP 2: Moisten a small sponge with water and a few drops of Lysol and place it in the jar. Cut a piece of cardboard to fit snugly inside the jar and place it on top of the sponge. Gently place a dry insect on top of the cardboard in the jar to keep it dry. Secure the jar's lid. Let it sit for about one day (it will absorb some of the moisture and become more pliable) before pinning the insect to your board.

PINNING INSECTS

STEP 3: When pinning insects to boards, you must use "insect pins," as common pins are too thick and will break the insects. Insect pins come in sizes from #0 (small) to #6 (large). A good size to start with is #2 or #3. They can be purchased from science supply stores.

Push an insect pin straight through the insect's thorax (fig. 2) until only ¼ inch (6 mm) remains above the insect's back (fig. 3). You can rest the insect on a piece of foam while you pin it. It helps to hold the insect by its thorax with your thumb and forefinger. Learning to pin your insects properly is very important (fig. 4).

(continued)

Fig. 4: Note the insect on the left is pinned correctly. The next insect is positioned too low on the pin. The third insect is not level on the pin. On the fourth pin, the insect is leaning.

STEP 4: If the insect is a butterfly, dragonfly, or other insect with wings, position the body in the V-shaped groove cut into your foam spreading board, or the cradle between the cardboard or corkboard pinning boards. After securing its body in the groove, gently spread its fore, or front, wings past its head until the trailing (back) edge of each wing is perpendicular to its body. Use a single pin behind the vein that runs down the leading (front) edge to secure it.

Next pull the hind wings forward until you can barely tuck them beneath the trailing edge of the forewings and pin them in place.

Pin strips of tracing paper tight over each pair of wings. Once secured, you can gently place pins in the strips of paper between the wings and remove the pins from the wings (fig. 5). The insect should be dry in four or five days. Never touch insects as you pin them.

STEP 5: Cut some labels from index cards (½ inch × ¾ inch, or 1 × 2 cm). When you remove the insect from the spreading board, place two labels on the pin beneath the insect (fig. 6). The first, or top, label will list the location, date, and your name. The second label will have the insect's common name.

Fig. 5: Pin strips of tracing paper over each pair of wings to hold them flat until they dry.

STEP 6: Handle the insect by the head of the pin and place it in your collection box. Insects should be arranged in your collection box by order, and the orders arranged in alphabetical order.

STORING YOUR COLLECTION

STEP 7: Cut three layers of corrugated cardboard or corkboard or one layer of foam to fit into the bottom of your storage box. Secure a mothball in one corner of the box with pins inserted in a triangle shape to discourage dermestid beetles from finding and eating your collected insects (fig. 7).

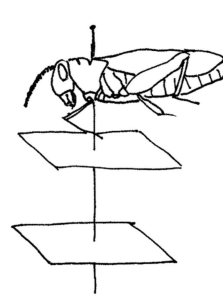

Fig. 6: Locator labels

BUG SCIENCE

A better alternative to using mothballs to preserve your collection is to regularly freeze it for one week every four months.

Fig. 7: Mothballs help preserve your insect collection.

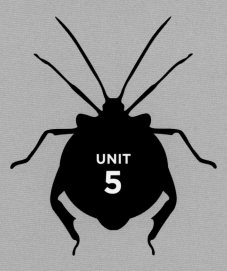

UNIT
5

THE MOST COMMON INSECT ORDERS

In this unit we will get to know a few insects in the orders with the largest number of insect species. This will also prepare us for further insect study in later labs.

ORDER COLEOPTERA: BEETLES

Beetle Strength Challenge

With more than 400,000 beetle species worldwide, it should be easy to find one for this activity: measuring a beetle's strength by how many pennies it can pull. The larger the beetle, the better. A Bess beetle, which makes a great insect pet, will work well.

Fig. 1: A Bess beetle pulling a "sled"

MATERIALS

- Your insect net (see Lab 4, page 28)
- 1 or 2 beetles, preferably bess beetles
- 1 critter keeper (if you want to keep them alive)
- String
- 2-×-3-inch (5 × 8 cm) piece of cardboard
- Hole punch
- Pennies
- Inexpensive postal scale
- Your field notebook
- Pencil

STEP 1: Collect one or two Bess beetles. Look under rotting logs in the woods. Wear boots and long pants, and step on top of a log before you roll it over to ensure there are no snakes under it. You may find other beetles on your search (see opposite).

STEP 2: When back indoors, gently tie a small string between the beetle's thorax and abdomen. Tie the other end of the string to a small (2- by 3-inch/5- by 8-cm) piece of cardboard with a hole punched in it. Place the beetle and its "sled" on a table with a tablecloth, which will give it better traction.

STEP 3: Once the beetle begins pulling, start stacking a few pennies on the cardboard. Continue adding pennies one at a time until the beetle is no longer able to pull the sled (fig. 1).

Hercules beetles

A weevil

BUG SCIENCE

The smallest animals seem to be the strongest! These beetles have exoskeletons that enable them to pull a relatively heavy load. The horned dung beetle is reportedly able to pull 1,000 times its own weight.

STEP 4: Use a postal scale to weigh the beetle, then the cardboard and pennies it was able to pull.

STEP 5: Calculate how many times the beetle's weight it could pull. For example, Bess bugs weigh about 0.05 ounces (1.5 grams); a penny weighs 0.09 ounces (2.5 grams).

- If a Bess beetle pulls 12 pennies, thats equal to about 30 grams (2.5 grams × 12).

- 30 grams divided by 1.5 grams (the Bess beetle's weight) = 20, which means it was able to pull 20 times its weight!

- How many times your weight do you think you can pull?

A stag beetle

The second largest group of insects includes more than 240,000 species—and possibly the most disliked: flies and mosquitoes. The order name *Diptera* is derived from the Greek word *di*, meaning "two," and *ptera*, referring to wings. In the first activity we take a close look at flies' wings; in the second, we look at a community service project for mosquito abatement.

MATERIALS

- A few flies
- Your insect net (see Lab 4, page 28)
- Your field notebook
- Pencil
- Small scissors
- Paper towel

Fig. 1: Robber fly with halteres.

Fig. 2: Horseflies, male (left) and female. Note that there is very little space between the male's eyes.

Studying Flies' Wings

Flies have a remarkable adaptation called halteres that enable them to fly with only two wings. Let's study them.

STEP 1: Collect a few hoverflies on flowers in the fall or horseflies in the spring to examine.

STEP 2: Notice that flies have only a single pair of wings. Below and behind their wings are short sticks resembling drumsticks called halteres (fig. 1). The current theory is that their gyroscopic action has a stabilizing function compensating for only having two wings. Sketch a picture of a fly in your field notebook including the halteres.

STEP 3: Snip off the halteres of a horsefly and observe its ability to fly.

Note: Female horseflies can bite so you may want to hold them with a paper towel. It is difficult to determine the gender of many adult insects; however, hoverfly and horsefly males have larger eyes than females. Look at the space between their eyes: The males have a very thin line while the females have more space (fig. 2). Examine those you collect and keep a record in your field notebook as to the gender of flies collected.

STEP 4: Record the results of your experiment in your field notebook.

BUG SCIENCE

Most insects have two pairs of wings. Flies are particularly interesting because they can fly with only one pair. To compensate for the lack of a second pair, flies are equipped with *halteres* (modified hind wings) that rotate during flight and have been thought to provide a stabilizing, or balancing, effect during flight. There is another small order, Strepsiptera, which has modified front wings instead.

Community Service: Mosquito Abatement

Conducting a community service activity to make your home and community inhospitable to mosquitoes will be of great help and importance to your community! You can make a difference in the health of your neighborhood.

MATERIALS

- Camera
- Appropriate clothing, such as a veil to wear over your hat and head, long-sleeve shirt, long pants, closed-toed shoes or boots
- Your field notebook
- Pencil
- Dipper on a stick for sampling mosquito larva in standing water

STEP 1: Begin by inspecting your yard or a nearby park for places where water stands after a rain. This is where mosquitoes breed. Check for plant saucers, plastic articles in the area, discarded tires, a birdbath, ditches that do not drain, air conditioner drains, low spots in the ground, clogged rain gutters, knot holes in trees, etc. (figs. 1 and 2). Document them with photos.

STEP 2: As you go, correct those that you can. You may need the assistance of an adult for some locations, such as rain gutters and city maintenance assistance for roadsides in high-traffic areas. List all that you found in your field notebook.

STEP 3: In standing water, look for mosquito eggs or rafts—a cluster of eggs that floats (fig. 3). Use your dipper stick.

STEP 4: Offer to check around your neighbors' houses, too (but only with their permission!). Their mosquitoes do not respect boundaries and will visit your yard, too (fig. 4).

STEP 5: Your good work will be noticed, and you can reduce mosquitoes in your neighborhood. Create a poster on mosquito abatement (eliminating and discouraging mosquitoes), if you wish, and ask whether you can display it in the local library or city hall. Volunteer to make public service announcements on the local radio or television station. If you have a local newspaper, write an article suggesting how others can make their homes and yards inhospitable to mosquitoes.

Fig. 1: Look for plant saucers as well as plants in standing water …

Fig. 2: … and stagnant pools of water.

Fig. 3: Look for a mosquito egg raft.

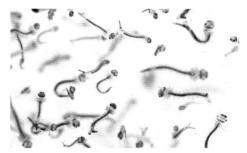

Fig. 4: Eliminate mosquito larvae in your neighborhood to keep it healthy for everyone.

BUG SCIENCE

The deadliest animals on the planet are mosquitoes, and the number of diseases vectored, or carried, by mosquitoes is growing. Mosquitoes have become an urban problem. They like our lifestyle that provides breeding puddles for them. Conduct a survey of the area around your home and neighborhood for places where water stands after a rain. Correct these problems by draining the water and preventing it from reoccurring.

Collecting and Studying Butterflies and Moths

Lepidoptera—175,000 species and still counting—includes moths and butterflies. There are probably fourteen moths to every butterfly, so you will probably collect more moths than butterflies. Moths are best collected in the evening.

For other butterfly projects, see Labs 35, 36, 37, and 38.

A monarch chrysalis is easy to recognize.

MATERIALS

- **Porch light or other outside light source (a flashlight should work, too)**
- **Magnifying glass**
- **1 dry collecting jar (see Lab 7, page 38)**
- **Your insect net (see Lab 4, page 28)**
- **Your field notebook**
- **Pencil**
- **Different colors of construction paper**
- **Hole punch**
- **Glue**
- **Camera**
- **Small ruler**

STEP 1: In the evening, turn on an outside light source and wait for the moths to approach. Touch a moth that is attracted to the light and examine the scales (modified flattened hairs) on your finger. Use your hand lens for a better look.

Note the disarranged scales in the electron microscope photo of butterfly scales (fig. 1). Scales have many functions: An interesting one is, because the scales are so easily shed, this enables moths to escape spiderwebs by shedding the scales that are stuck. Throw a couple moths into spiderwebs and check to see if this is true. Record your results in your field notebook.

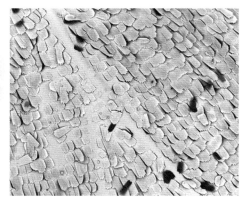
Fig. 1: Electron microscope photo of butterfly scales. Moths have similar properties.

Fig. 2: Eastern tiger swallowtail butterfly.

Fig. 3: What type of moth did you collect? Was it a sphinx moth like this one?

STEP 2: Scales also give moths and butterflies their colors. Make lots of different colors of construction paper holes. Arrange and glue them together to create a picture of a butterfly or moth using the holes as scales, maybe like this eastern tiger swallowtail butterfly (fig. 2). Take a picture of your creation.

STEP 3: Collect a moth (fig. 3) and examine its proboscis—a coiled drinking straw under its head used to sip nectar. Gently extend it to see how long it is.

Nectaries are found at the base of flowers. Different moths use different flowers depending on the depth of the nectaries and the length of their proboscises. Collect a moth visiting a flower and measure the length of its proboscis and the depth of the flower's nectaries. Record your findings.

Fig. 4: Butterflies puddling.

STEP 4: At night, in a 2-hour period, count as many moths as you can. Record your results.

STEP 5: During the day in spring or summer, in a 2-hour period, count as many butterflies as you can. Did you see any puddling (fig. 4)? Record your results.

BUG SCIENCE

Touching a moth on an outside wall near a light will leave a lot of gray scales on your finger. Many moths have colorful wings that resemble butterfly wings. Some moths have eyespots that look like owl eyes and are useful for scaring possible predators! Look through a moth field guide and sketch a picture of a moth in your field notebook. Punch out more colorful paper holes and glue the "scales" into your sketch to resemble the insects.

A potter wasp.

The fourth largest order, Hymenoptera includes more than 150,000 species, including wasps, bees, and ants. For this activity, we focus on wasps, specifically potter wasps.

For other Hymenoptera projects, see Labs 32 and 33.

Potter Wasps

Potter, or mason, wasps create incredible structures that look like a pot "thrown" on a potter's wheel! The female collects prey as food for her larvae. The adults feed on nectar. The marble-size mud nest appears to be somewhat resistant to rain, which suggests an experiment. The hypothesis you will be testing is, "The wasp nest will not dissolve at the same rate as the one you create." This may be true because the wasps may have added waterproofing chemicals from their saliva.

MATERIALS

- Garden trowel
- Cup
- 2 pencils with erasers on top, 1 for the nest and 1 for recording in your notebook
- 2 small jars or bottles with lids
- Your field notebook

STEP 1: Be on the lookout for a potter wasp nest on plant stems and leaves in the garden or window screens (fig. 1). Wait until you see a hole in the side of the nest, indicating the wasp has emerged, and gently remove the nest.

STEP 2: Carefully examine the mud used by the wasp. Look around near where you found the nest for mud or soil the same color. Collect a small sample. Mix it with a little water and make a pot by flattening and folding it into a hollow hemisphere over a pencil eraser.

STEP 3: Gently remove it and round it in your hands. It should be hollow and close to the same size as your collected nest. The walls of the nest you create should be as thin as the wasp's nest. Gently cut a hole, similar in size to the wasp's nest. Let it dry for about one week.

STEP 4: When your nest is dry, place the real wasp's nest and your replica in two small bottles that are the same size.

Fig. 1: A potter wasp nest.

Add an equal amount of water to each bottle. Record when you placed the real and replica nests in the bottles of water. Place the caps on the bottles. Each day invert both bottles and leave them sitting right-side up on a shelf or countertop.

STEP 5: Continue flipping the bottles each day until the nests begin to dissolve. Record the date. Which dissolved first—the one produced by the wasp, or yours?

BUG SCIENCE

Potter wasps are beneficial to have around, as they are predators of garden pests.

Fig. 1: Aphids

Insect Mouthparts

All bugs are insects, but not all insects are bugs. Insects in this group, or order—more than 80,000 species—are notorious for being extremely destructive to commercial crops. A useful characteristic of insects in this order is their mouthpart that utilizes strawlike structures. This activity will focus on insect mouthparts. The variety of mouthparts enables insects to have extremely diverse diets!

Fig. 2: A wheel bug

Fig. 3: Milkweed bugs

MATERIALS

- **Magnifying glass**
- **Your field notebook**
- **Pencil**

STEP 1: Inspect several goldenrod plants (search online for a picture if you're unsure what they look like) when they are blooming. Look for green or red aphids (fig. 1) with their proboscises stuck in the vascular tissue and their posteriors in the air.

STEP 2: Compare their proboscises with the mouthparts of the insects in figs. 2 to 5. Their functions are related to the foods they eat. What differences or similarities do you see?

STEP 3: Examine several insects in each order with your hand lens and sketch pictures of their mouthparts on a page in your field notebook.

Fig. 4: A stinkbug

Fig. 5: A leaf-footed bug

BUG SCIENCE

The diversity of insect mouths is astounding. Beetles, earwigs, and mantids have chewing mouthparts. Lacewings and antlions have a hooked mandible for capturing prey. Flies sponge up their food. Butterflies have siphoning tubes coiled under their heads until they need a drink.

And, finally, only insects in Hemiptera are known as "true bugs." "BWG," or "BUGGE," were ancient old Middle English words for spirits or ghosts thought responsible for the red welts that mysteriously appeared on people in the morning. The culprits were bed bugs with piercing, sucking mouthparts. Today, all bugs with piercing, sucking mouthparts are grouped in the Hemipteran order and in entomological vernacular still referred to as "bugs" or "true bugs." So, while all bugs are insects, not all insects are bugs and only hemipterans are "true bugs."

A caddisfly

Caddisfly Cases

Caddisflies—12,000 species of them—are stonemasons, log-cabin builders, and net makers. Caddisflies are common in streams and ponds. Caddisfly cases are so beautiful they're sometimes used to make jewelry.

Fig. 1: Search for caddisfly cases.

Fig. 2: Can you find a stick caddisfly case like this one?

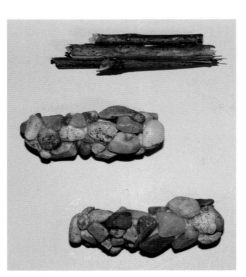

Fig. 3: Your completed caddisfly cases will look like this.

BUG SCIENCE

Caddisflies build oblong cases of pebbles cemented together, or twigs stacked reminiscent of a log cabin. The aquatic net makers produce very small webs useful for collecting prey in streams. Eggs are usually laid in gelatinous masses attached to rocks or stems. After hatching, the caddisfly larva begins collecting grains of sand and cementing them into a case around its body. The front is open to enable it to crawl around in search of food. After the larva stage the pupa remains in the case until it emerges as an adult. When it is time, the pupa cuts open its case, swims to the surface, crawls up a stem, sheds its skin, spreads it wings, and flies. Its life is short, so it must find a mate within a few days.

MATERIALS

- **Magnifying glass**
- **Your field notebook**
- **Pencil**
- **Several small sticks about ⅛ inch (3 mm) in diameter and 1 inch (2.5 cm) long**
- **Glue**
- **Small colorful pebbles that you've gathered**

STEP 1: If you live near a stream, search around rocks and sandy bottoms for caddisfly cases (fig. 1). Stick cases (fig. 2) may be found in very slow-moving water or ponds. Sometimes you will find cases in clusters.

STEP 2: Examine the cases you find, looking at the individual pebbles or sticks. Often caddisflies select surprisingly attractive or valuable stones.

STEP 3: Sketch pictures of the cases in your field notebook.

STEP 4: Make a caddisfly case by selecting a small stick, then gluing very small pebbles to cover the stick completely (fig. 3).

Insect Interactions

There are innumerable interactions among the orders, and this is a dependable one to observe. Lacewing (Neuroptera) larvae eat ants (Hymenoptera) that herd aphids (Hemiptera). Ants enjoy the sweet honeydew the aphids excrete and will even "milk," or stroke, the aphids for it. The ants are farming the aphids, corralling them, and even moving them to fresh plants.

Fig. 1: A green lacewing

MATERIALS

- **Magnifying glass**
- **Your field notebook**
- **Pencil**

STEP 1: Find a field of blooming golden-rod, sunflowers, Queen Anne's lace, or corn, and look closely at the stems for the green aphids, ants, and lacewings (fig. 1). You will enjoy watching their interactions.

STEP 2: Look for the green lacewings that may be nearby, and their larvae that look like very small alligators until they have camouflaged themselves (fig. 2). People often think the lichens on their trees have come alive when, in fact, the lacewing larvae have camouflaged themselves with pieces of lichen and other plant material! This is a real-world example of the Aesop fable where a clever wolf (green lacewing larva) donned a sheepskin (dead aphids or lichen) and snuck past the shepherd (ant) for a tasty meal (aphid)!

The ants actively herd the aphids, protecting them and moving them to new sites to feed (fig. 3). The lacewing larvae will be darting around making a meal of the aphids. You may even see aphids give birth to babies.

STEP 3: Record your observations and sketch pictures in your field notebook.

Can you find any lacewing eggs like these?

Fig. 2: Look for lacewing larvae—they look like small alligators.

Fig. 3: Watch for ants herding the aphids.

BUG SCIENCE

Green lacewing larvae are voracious predators of insect pests including aphids, thrips, whiteflies, leafhoppers, and other plant pests. Lacewings lay their eggs close to aphids actively feeding on plants such as goldenrod. Lacewing eggs are on the tops of thin stalks. When their eggs hatch the alligatorlike larvae binge on aphids!

Fig. 1: A delicate damselfly.

Dragonfly Inspection

Dragonflies and damselflies (5,900 species) are a little difficult to collect until you learn their flight plan—back and forth, as in a search pattern. Almost anywhere there is water, you will see these insects. Observing mites on the dragonflies is easy—collect a few, then release them when you're done with the experiment.

MATERIALS

- **Your field notebook**
- **Pencil**
- **Your insect net (see Lab 4, page 28)**

STEP 1: Find a location with water where damselflies (fig. 1) or dragonflies (fig. 2) are active, and watch. Get a good look at the coloration of the one you are watching so you can recognize it when it returns.

STEP 2: Wait for it to return. Did it make a large circle and reappear from the same direction? Or, did it come back from the direction it flew to? Record your observations in your field notebook.

STEP 3: Now that you know, get ready and catch it!

STEP 4: Inspect your insects closely because they often have mites (fig. 3). When you notice mites or other abnormal characteristics, make a note in your field notebook.

Fig. 2: Observe the coloration of the dragonfly you've spotted. It may even be camouflaged on a plant.

Fig. 3: Inspect your dragonfly closely for mites, as you see here.

Termite Circus

Termites, Isoptera, (1,900 species) share a common ancestor with cockroaches, Blattodea, (4,600 species) and mantids (2,400 species). Homeowners dread termites because they feed on wood and wood byproducts. Termites use chemicals that attract other insects and guide them to food sources. In this activity, we use pens whose ink has a component that mimics the trail pheromones of termites to create a termite circus!

A termite

MATERIALS

- Trowel
- 20 to 30 termites
- Plastic container with lid
- Sharp object for punching holes in the container's lid
- 10 ballpoint pens, some with blue ink and some with black ink
- Paper
- Your field notebook
- Pencil

STEP 1: Termites are common in rotting logs. Roll one over and inspect it for termites. Collect termites, along with some of the wood they have been living in, in the plastic container. Punch a few holes in the lid for ventilation and place it on the container.

STEP 2: Draw concentric circles on a piece of paper with each of the pens, leaving at least 3 or 4 inches (8 to 10 cm) inside the innermost circle.

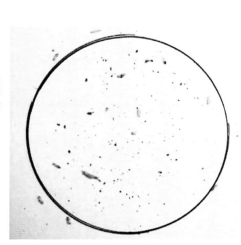

Fig. 1: Amaze your friends with your termite circus.

STEP 3: Place several termites in the center of the circles and observe their movement. When they find the ink that mimics their trail pheromone, they will follow it around and around. Some may go in the other direction and some may change direction (fig. 1).

Will they cross a paper bridge with an ink line across it? Make a paper bridge and see.

STEP 4: If none of the termites follows any of the ink lines, find different ink pens to try. Record this activity in your field notebook.

STEP 5: Amaze your friends with your "trained" termite circus.

BUG SCIENCE

- Ants and termites are often confused for each other—ants have bent antennae, while termites have straight, beadlike antennae.

- Termites have an elongated abdomen.

- Termite and ant swarms are a great concern, and many people have difficulty telling them apart when they have wings. The front and back wings of a termite are roughly equal in size and shape, whereas the front wings on an ant (when they are winged) are much larger than the hind wings.

- Have trouble exterminating cockroaches? Remember: Some were here before the dinosaurs! A popular bug festival activity is the Madagascar hissing cockroach race.

Termites are dreaded by homeowners because of the major damage they can cause.

A cockroach

INSECT ORDER SAMPLING

In this activity, we practice a technique for sampling, or counting, the largest four orders by size and determine the percentage of insects in each order. We also consider whether a larger sample size gives a more accurate representation of insects living in a particular habitat.

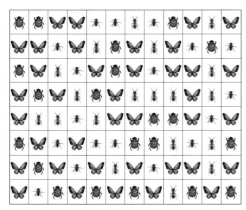

Insect sampling board (see page 135 for full size)

MATERIALS

- 1 bag of dried beans
- Insect Sampling Board (see page 135)
- Your field notebook
- Pencil
- Calculator

STEP 1: Toss 20 beans onto the insect sampling board (see page 135) and count the number of Lepidoptera, butterflies and moths (fig. 1); Diptera, flies and mosquitoes (fig. 2); Coleoptera, beetles (fig. 3); and Hymenoptera, bees, ants, and wasps (fig. 4). Record your results in your field notebook.

Now calculate the percentages of each: When you toss 20 beans onto the board, if 8 land in "beetles," that equals 40 percent.

- 100 percent ÷ 20 beans × 8 that landed in beetles = 40 percent

STEP 2: Repeat the sample with 40 beans. Count the number that landed in each order and record your results. Calculate the percentage of each order sampled.

STEP 3: Now repeat the sample with 60 beans and count the number that landed in each order. Calculate the percentage of each order sampled. Create a table in your field notebook like the one shown on page 89 and record your results.

STEP 4: Based on your observation, do you think larger sample sizes give a more accurate picture of the population size? If the insects had been scattered in the woods instead of corralled on a table, would that have influenced your results?

SAMPLE SIZE	COLEOPTERA (BEETLES) NUMBER & PERCENT	DIPTERA (FLIES) NUMBER & PERCENT	HYMENOPTERA (BEES, ANTS & WASPS) NUMBER & PERCENT	LEPIDOPTERA (MOTHS & BUTTERFLIES) NUMBER & PERCENT
20 BEANS				
40 BEANS				
60 BEANS				

Fig. 1: Imperial moth, order Lepidoptera

Fig. 2: Crane fly, order Diptera

BUG SCIENCE

Sampling techniques are used to determine the abundance of insects in different orders within a specific area. When you are searching for insects outdoors, you can test your results by gradually increasing the size of the area you sample.

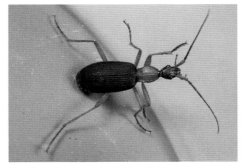
Fig. 3: Blister beetle, order Coleoptera

Fig. 4: Bee, order Hymenoptera

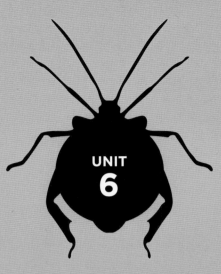

OTHER ARTHROPOD ADVENTURES

Insects are the most abundant arthropods, but there are others you will encounter and enjoy getting to know. *Arthropod* means "jointed foot." These insects have segmented bodies of more than one part; some have many legs, an exoskeleton, and are cold blooded. Arthropods include insects, spiders, centipedes, millipedes, scorpions, ticks, shrimp, barnacles, crabs, and many more.

CENTIPEDES & MILLIPEDES: SPEED & DIET

In this lab, we examine two common myriapods—centipedes and millipedes—and determine how fast they can move or run. Is their locomotion, including number of legs, related to their diet?

MATERIALS

- Critter keeper
- Camera that records video
- Small stick
- String
- Ruler
- Your field notebook
- Pencil
- Lab partner
- Timer

Young entomologists seeing how fast centipedes can run!

Fig. 1: Redheaded centipede with two legs per body segment

Fig. 2: Millipede with four legs per body segment

BUG SCIENCE

Centipedes have two legs per segment and millipedes have four legs per segment. Centipedes—without as many legs to coordinate—can run much faster than millipedes. This enables them to be carnivorous and chase down their food. Millipedes are herbaceous, or plant eaters. Having to coordinate four legs per segment results in slower movement for them. Fortunately, their food does not run from them and their legs enable them to cling to the plants they eat.

MEASURING CENTIPEDE SPEED

STEP 1: Find a centipede (fig. 1) and coax it into your critter keeper. Use your camera to record a video while you touch a centipede in a critter keeper with a small stick. They are very fast and deliver a surprising bite—keep your hands out of their reach! Watch your video and lay a piece of string over the path it ran. Measure the string. Play the video again and measure how long it lasts in seconds. Divide the number of inches (cm) of the string by the number of seconds to determine how many inches (cm) the centipede moved per second. Record your results in your field notebook.

MEASURING MILLIPEDE SPEED

STEP 2: Find a millipede (fig. 2) and place it in your critter keeper. Millipedes won't respond to being touched by a stick, so you may need to wait until yours is actually crawling to do this experiment. Because a millipede is much slower, you can place the string on its path behind it as it crawls. Be sure to measure the time it is crawling. Measure the string that represents the path and divide the number of inches (cm) by the number of seconds your millipede crawled to determine how many inches (cm) it moved per second.

A COMPARISON

STEP 3: Get a lab partner to time you as you run across the room as fast as you can. Now, crawl across the room as fast as you can while your friend times you. It is easier to see that the (carnivorous) centipede with only two legs per segment can chase down its prey faster than a millipede with multiple legs per segment. The millipede is a plant eater, and it is a good thing it does not need the speed of the centipede to catch its dinner!

WHAT DO ISOPODS LIKE?

Isopods, or rolypolies, are commonly available and easy to use in experiments. You can collect isopods for experiments from under rocks, logs, leaves, mulch, flowerpots, and pieces of bark—or even a cardboard box left in the yard. In this activity, we determine a rolypoly's preferences for light or dark, and moist or dry habitats.

A sow bug (above) and pill bug (top). Sow bugs cannot roll into a ball, but pill bugs can.

MATERIALS

FOR WET VS. DRY ENVIRONMENTS
- **Petri dish or small plastic container**
- **Paper towel**
- **Scissors**
- **Timer**

FOR LIGHT VS. DARK ENVIRONMENTS
- **Small piece of cardboard or index card**
- **Petri dish and isopods (from wet vs. dry experiment, listed above)**
- **Your field notebook**
- **Pencil**

Fig. 1: In a clear plastic kitchen container with a lid, place your isopods in the center of the paper towel with one side moistened.

Fig. 2: Isopods, like shrimp, must remain moist for gas exchange to occur, and so prefer the dark moist area.

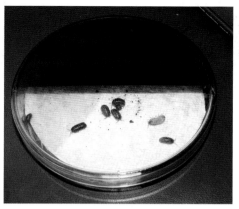

Fig. 3: Cover your isopods (black paper, tented cardboard, or painting the lid a dark color all work).

ROLYPOLIES: WET OR DRY ENVIRONMENTS?

STEP 1: Cut pieces of paper towel to the size of the container. If the container is round, place the paper towel in it and moisten one half of the towel. If the container is square or rectangular, place pieces on both sides of the container with a little space between them.

STEP 2: Release the isopods in the area between the wet and dry areas (fig. 1). Give them 15 minutes to learn their way around and decide which side to remain on.

STEP 3: Where did they go? Isopods are kin to shrimp and use book lungs (respiratory organs) to breathe. They must remain moist for gas exchange to occur. Record your results in your field notebook.

ROLYPOLIES: LIGHT OR DARK?

STEP 1: Place a piece of cardboard over half of the container. Place isopods in the center of the container—not under the cardboard (fig. 2).

STEP 2: Place the roly-poly experiment in the sun.

STEP 3: Monitor to see whether they enjoy the sun or seek shelter under the cardboard (fig. 3). Record your observations in your field notebook.

BUG SCIENCE

Rolypolies are not insects; they are land-based crustaceans and kin to shrimp and crawfish. They breathe with modified gills (book lungs) that need moisture to function. They thrive anywhere it is damp and dark.

Having a pet spider that lives outdoors near your house makes an incredible companion! Spiders are fun to watch and feed, and they also trap undesirable bugs. The black and yellow garden spider is a beneficial arachnid to have around, and, if you're lucky, her spiderling descendants will continue trapping small insects and entertaining you and visitors for years!

Fig. 1: A black and yellow garden spider behind her stabilimentum (zigzag)

MATERIALS
- **Your field notebook**
- **Pencil**
- **Camera**

STEP 1: Look for a spider to adopt (fig. 1). They are often found under the eaves of houses or other buildings. If you can't find the black and yellow garden spider, look for another type.

STEP 2: Periodically, but not too often, collect and throw live insects into her web (fig. 2).

STEP 3: Make careful observations and take photos of bugs trapped, or thrown, into her web, the smaller male's appearance, egg sacs, etc. Sketch her web in your field notebook. Date your observations.

STEP 4: There is more to discover—continue making observations over time and record them in your field notebook.

Fig. 2: Feeding an *Argiope* spider

BUG SCIENCE

The black and yellow garden spider (just one of many orb weavers that builds circular webs) has a wide distribution, and there are orb weavers with similar characteristics in close habitation with humans worldwide. When disturbed they can bite, but their venom is relatively harmless to humans and feels like a bee sting.

Their webs can be up to 5 or 6 feet (152 to 183 cm) in diameter and have zigzag "stabilimentum" (web decoration) sometimes described as scribbling. The female enthusiastically vibrates her web, possibly to warn you off, to entangle a meal, or discourage predators. The male will build a small web nearby and periodically pluck the female's larger web to get her attention.

Wolf spiders are relatively common, large spiders. The males are smaller; the females are very protective of their spiderlings. The young ride on their mothers' backs. This is what you will be on the lookout for in this activity.

MATERIALS

- **Your field notebook**
- **Pencil**

STEP 1: Walk around your neighborhood and ask neighbors to report back to you if they spot any spiderwebs. When you find a wolf spider that looks like it has a hairy back, look more closely—you may be seeing many spiderlings (fig. 1)! With her keen eyesight, Momma Wolf Spider will be watching you, too. It is common to find them in homes, but don't hurt them.

STEP 2: Very slowly and gently tap her with your finger or a pencil to dislodge a few spiderlings. They will run around and she will freeze, waiting to make sure it is safe before continuing.

STEP 3: When she decides you are not a threat, she will stand up tall on her legs signaling for her spiderlings to climb back on, and then she will be on her way. This is incredible to watch. Describe your observations in your field notebook.

STEP 4: If you have observed this indoors, take a piece of paper and gently scoop the mother and her spiderlings into a cup or bowl and take them outside to release.

Fig. 1: A wolf spider with spiderlings on her back

BUG SCIENCE

Wolf spiders are active nocturnal (nighttime) hunters and have eight eyes—two of which are large and prominent. Their eyes are arranged in three rows. Shining a flashlight into its eyes will produce notable eyeshine, or reflection. They do not spin webs, and live and hunt alone. These spiders can be brown, gray, black, or tan and their camouflage protects them. They are reluctant to bite, and bites typically exhibit only minor swelling and redness. They carry their egg sacs underneath or attached to their spinnerets (thread-producing organs), and are very protective.

These guys are common enough that you will enjoy amazing your friends with your Opilione (order name) wrangling ability! This activity is best done in front of a large audience of your friends. While they're all backing off, telling you how "poisonous" these "spiders" are, you can share what you have learned.

Fig. 1: A granddaddy longlegs under a leaf.

MATERIALS

- **Small stick**
- **Your field notebook**
- **Pencil**
- **Black light (inexpensive black light flashlights are available at big box stores)**

STEP 1: Find a granddaddy longlegs (fig. 1). Go ahead, pick it up (fig. 2), and let it walk around on your hands. Watch for some defensive behaviors—bobbing or vibrating their bodies or playing dead.

STEP 2: They have scent glands and, if they should use them (they have a smell), collect some on a stick and look for an ant trail. Draw a line across the trail with this secretion and see if it deters the ants. Record your observations in your field notebook.

Fig. 2: Go ahead—don't be afraid to hold a granddaddy longlegs.

Fig. 3: A black light flashlight. **Do not** look directly at the light from a black light flashlight.

STEP 3: In the unfortunate event your Opilione loses a leg, instruct those with you to watch the leg carefully. "Pacemakers" located in the long femur repeatedly signal the muscles to extend the leg, and the leg relaxes between signals. Some think this may distract predators.

STEP 4: Some species produce a fluorescence when exposed to ultraviolet, or black, light. Use a black light flashlight to find out (fig. 3). Does yours?

SAFETY FIRST!

NEVER LOOK directly into the light made by a black light flashlight. The ultraviolet (UV) light may damage your eyes!

BUG SCIENCE

The Opiliones are an order of arachnids that, in recent years, have developed an undeserved bad reputation. The harvestmen or daddy longlegs, as they are commonly called, are not spiders and are not harmful to humans.

Next time you have a seafood dinner, eat the bugs, examine their parts, and sketch them! Crawfish, crabs, shrimp, and lobster are all arthropods. *Entomophagy* is the practice of eating insects, and about 80 percent of the people on Earth eat insects!

MATERIALS

• **Your field notebook**

• **Pencil**

STEP 1: Keep a record of the arthropods, including shrimp, lobster, crab, and crawfish, that you eat in your field notebook. Include a sketch of each.

STEP 2: Describe the experience and the flavor.

Fig. 1: A cricket lollipop

Fig. 2: Mealworm rice treats

Fig. 3: Dr. Guyton (the author) cooking mealworms

STEP 3: Start a list in your field notebook of insects and other arthropods you see for sale as human food. Insect zoos, bug festivals, and bug camps often feature edible insects. Novelty stores often sell suckers with arthropods and other insects, including crunchy crickets, chocolate-covered crickets, and others, imbedded right inside (fig. 1). You might also see mealworm rice treats (fig. 2) and insect brittle! When you try an edible insect, make notes in your field notebook, including your reaction and its taste, along with a sketch.

STEP 4: Contact the entomology department at a university near you to see if they have a professor or specialist involved in *entomophagy*—the practice of humans eating insects (fig. 3). There may be events in which you can participate. If no university is nearby, many novelty stores in malls sell insect treats and they are also readily available online for you to try.

BUG SCIENCE

The Food and Agriculture Organization of the United Nations has identified more than 1,900 species of insects that have been used for food. Hunger affects almost a billion people worldwide, and insects will be part of the solution.

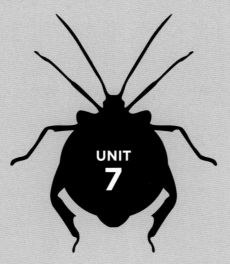

BUG ART & SCIENCE PROJECTS

Activities in this unit are a blend of science and art. It starts with a science experiment followed by an art project that uses the same techniques wasps use to make a nest. Making a yellow jacket trap is a functional activity and one that shows how to trap yellow jackets and other insects. This is an example of integrated pest management— no pesticides are needed in a physical trap. To complete the unit, we make a butterfly water feature with which to conduct a science experiment.

LAB 32

PAPIER-MÂCHÉ WASP NEST

Wasps were making paper before humans knew how to write! When we started making paper we made it just like wasps do—grinding wood to a pulp, adding water and chemicals, and flattening or shaping the mixture. Let's make a paper wasp's nest.

MATERIALS

- 1 sheet of newspaper
- 2 small bowls
- ½ cup (64 g) cornstarch, plus more as needed
- ¼ cup (60 ml) water, plus more as needed
- 1 tablespoon (18 g) salt
- Blender
- 12 unsharpened hexagonal pencils, plus more if needed (the more pencils, the larger the nest)
- 2 rubber bands

STEP 1: Tear the newspaper into small pieces, or put it through a paper shredder.

STEP 2: In a small bowl, stir together the cornstarch, water, and salt (to prevent molding).

STEP 3: In a blender, combine the newspaper pieces and cornstarch mixture. Blend until it has a thick pasty texture (fig. 1). If it is too thick, add more water; if too thin, add more cornstarch dissolved in water, or add more paper.

A wasp using wood fiber to make her nest.

Fig. 1: Your papier-mâché mixture will look like this.

Fig. 2: Pencils with their paper-coated tips

Fig. 3: Gather the pencils and secure them with rubber bands.

Fig. 4: Gently remove the pencils from the dry nest one at a time.

BUG SCIENCE

Wasps make their nests from old wood. If you follow one from the nest while it is being built you will discover it landing on exposed wood where it will tear off a small piece. All the way back to its nest it chews the wood (much as paper mills grind up wood to make paper for us) and adds saliva (as the mills add chemicals) to what will become paper. When the wasp reaches the nest, it adds the moist ball of wood pulp to the nest. It then taps it into the shape of a hexagon, with six sides, because that shape can hold the greatest amount of contents with the least amount of materials used in its construction.

STEP 4: Pour about ¾ inch (2 cm) of the mixture into your small bowl. Using your hands, begin coating the bottom inch (2.5 cm) of the pencils with a thin layer of the mixture. Balance the paper-tipped pencils across the top of a second bowl while you apply paper pulp to the rest of your pencils (fig. 2). Carefully gather the pencils so their erasers are together and gently squeeze them to stick together. Carefully place 2 rubber bands around the pencils to hold them together (fig. 3).

STEP 5: Allow the wasp nest to air-dry for two days. Alternatively, you can microwave the nest for 2 minutes at 50 percent power, check, and continue in 2-minutes increments, checking after each, until dry. A warm oven can be used after it has been turned off to speed drying; it will take about 2 hours. Don't rush the drying. Once the nest begins to feel dry, periodically wiggle the grouped pencils so, eventually, the nest can be easily removed from the pencils.

Fig. 5: A finished wasp's nest.

STEP 6: When the paper wasp's nest is dry, remove the pencils by holding the nest and removing the pencils one at a time (fig. 4). Let the nest air-dry for a few more hours (fig. 5).

LAB 33
YELLOW JACKET TRAP: INTEGRATED PEST MANAGEMENT (IPM)

MATERIALS

- Scissors
- 2-liter soda bottle
- Glue gun and glue sticks
- Empty pill bottle or small cup
- Hole punch
- Coat hanger or 10-inch (25 cm) picture hanging wire
- 1 pint (480 ml) jar with a lid
- ½ cup (120 ml) water
- ½ cup (120 ml) apple cider vinegar
- ¼ cup (50 g) sugar
- Your field notebook
- Pencil

Yellow jackets are unwelcome pests. IPM, or integrated pest management, is an effective and environmentally sensitive approach to pest management that relies on common-sense practices, not pesticides. In this activity, we take advantage of our knowledge of what yellow jackets and other flying pests eat to trap them! The trap you create will work even when you are not around.

STEP 1: Identify a spot where you've seen yellow jackets.

STEP 2: Use scissors to cut the top off a 2-liter soda bottle (fig. 1) at the point where the curved side meets the vertical side. Discard the cap.

STEP 3: Glue the pill bottle or small cup into the bottom of the bottle.

STEP 4: Push the soda bottle's top, upside down, into the bottle.

STEP 5: About ¾ inch (2 cm) from the top, use a hole punch to punch a hole through both plastic parts on each side. Attach the coat hanger wire or picture hanging wire through the holes, bending the ends up inside the holes, to hold the two pieces together and serve as a hanger for the trap (fig. 2).

STEP 6: In the jar, combine the water, vinegar, and sugar. Secure the lid and shake vigorously. Pour the mixture into the trap. Place a piece of banana peel into the pill bottle.

STEP 7: Hang your trap where you have seen yellow jackets. This trap has one entrance. Once they fly in they cannot fly out and will eventually drown in the liquid in the bottom.

STEP 8: Rinse off a couple dead yellow jackets and other insects that were attracted to the trap and save them for your collection. Record the results of your experiments with the yellow jacket trap.

Fig. 1: Cut the top off a 2-liter soda bottle.

Fig. 2: To complete the trap, put the top upside down into the bottom of the bottle, attach a wire for hanging, and place the bait inside the trap.

BUG SCIENCE

IPM, which focuses on pest control practices that are the most economical and pose the least possible hazard for people, property, and the environment, should be used before resorting to chemicals.

You can use this IPM project to trap other insects: Use small pieces of meat to attract flies; sweets for hornets; 1 table-spoon (12 g) of yeast, ⅓ cup (75 g) of brown sugar, and 1 cup (240 ml) of water and wrap the bottle in black paper for mosquitoes; vinegar for fruit flies; and an LED (light-emitting diode) taped to a battery and placed in the bottom of the bottle for attracting other insects. Record the results of each insect you used the trap to collect, listing how many of each insect were collected and what you used for bait.

SAFETY FIRST!

Caution: Collecting bees and wasps, including yellow jackets, requires important safety precautions. When alarmed, they can attack in great numbers and can tag or mark you with pheromones, or chemicals, that label you as an enemy.

A fly on a carnivorous pitcher plant

MATERIALS

- **Photocopier**
- **Pitcher plant template (see page 137)**
- **Construction paper**
- **Scissors**
- **Tape**
- **14-inch (35 cm) piece of string**
- **Stapler (optional)**
- **Plastic fly**

Carnivorous plants live in nitrogen-poor soil and compensate for this deficiency by attracting insects and breaking down their bodies for the nitrogen. In this activity, we make a game that involves a paper carnivorous pitcher plant connected to a plastic fly. By swinging the pitcher plant, you can catch the fly in the pitcher—with a little practice!

STEP 1: On a copier, enlarge the pitcher plant template (fig. 1; see page 137 for the template) so it fills a whole 8½-inch × 11-inch (21 × 28 cm) page of construction paper.

STEP 2: Curl the cutout template into an ice cream cone shape and tape it in place (fig. 2).

STEP 3: Tape or staple the string to the top front of the pitcher, tie a plastic fly to the other end of the string, and curl the lid, just a little, over the pitcher (fig. 3).

STEP 4: To play the game, swing the pitcher so the fly becomes airborne, and then catch the fly in the pitcher plant!

Fig. 1: Pitcher plant template with other supplies

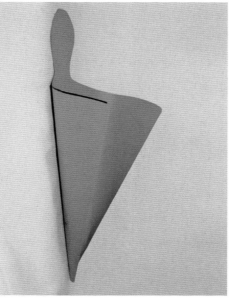

Fig. 2: Curl the template into a cone shape; tape it in place.

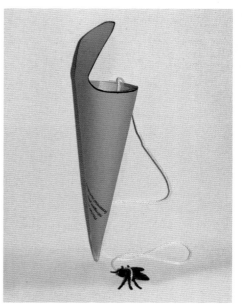

Fig. 3: Tape the string to the funnel at the top front of the template, and tie the fly on the other end.

BUG SCIENCE

Ants, flies, and other insects are attracted to the sweet smell of the pitcher plant's nectar. Hairs inside the pitcher all point down, and insects have great difficulty climbing back over the hairs and out of the plant. The only way for them to go is down. Enzymes in the plant dissolve the connecting tissue between the insect's exoskeleton pieces to access the nitrogen needed by the carnivorous plant. There are some insects, such as the pitcher plant moth caterpillar, that are adapted to crawling around on top of the hairs and living inside the pitcher plant—they are not digested by the plant.

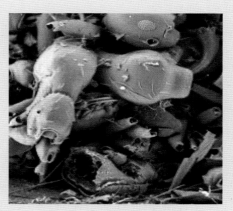

This electron microscope photograph shows ant body parts inside a pitcher plant.

BUTTERFLY WATERING STATION

In this lab, you'll experiment with a butterfly species that's common in your area to determine whether they're more attracted to a black silhouette of their shape, or to one in their dominant color. We used the shape of an eastern tiger swallowtail, which is predominantly yellow with black markings.

MATERIALS

- Protective work gloves (Kevlar or fisherman's)
- Aluminum soda can
- Sturdy scissors
- Markers
- Photocopy of butterfly shape (optional)
- Grade 0000 steel wool
- Acrylic or spray paint in black and another color (we used yellow)
- Hammer and nail
- 2 wooden dowels, 2 to 3 feet (61 to 91 cm) long
- 2 thumbtacks
- Field notebook
- Pencil

STEP 1: Wearing protective gloves, use the scissors to carefully cut away the top and bottom of an aluminum soda can. Cut the can into a single strip (fig. 1).

STEP 2: On the inside of the can, use the marker to draw two outlines of a butterfly that's common to your yard. You can also photocopy a photograph of the butterfly, cut it out, and trace its shape onto the can (fig. 2).

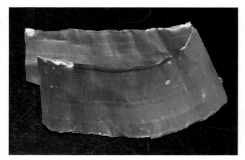

Fig. 1: Carefully cut an aluminum can into a strip.

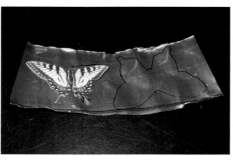

Fig. 2: Sketch or trace the butterfly's shape on the inside of the can.

Fig. 3: Paint the butterflies; let dry. Make a hole in the center of each with a hammer and nail.

Fig. 4: Attach each butterfly to the top of a dowel with a thumbtack.

BUG SCIENCE

Research suggests butterflies recognize and are attracted to the shape of other butterflies of their species.

STEP 3: Carefully cut out the butterflies. Sand the inside with steel wool.

STEP 4: Paint one butterfly black, and the other the dominant color of your chosen butterfly.

STEP 5: Make a hole in the center of each butterfly by hammering a nail through it (fig. 3). Attach each butterfly to a dowel with a thumbtack (fig. 4).

STEP 6: Experiment with each silhouette in turn at a water feature (see opposite), or make two sets of butterflies and place them simultaneously around two separate water features or in different locations in your yard or garden.

STEP 7: Use your field notebook to keep a record of the butterflies attracted to each silhouette to see if you can answer the question: Are butterflies attracted to black butterfly silhouettes, or colored ones?

SAFETY FIRST!

You'll need adult supervision and help to:

• Cut the aluminum soda can with scissors

• Make holes in the center of each butterfly with a hammer and nail

REARING BUTTERFLIES & BUTTERFLY MIGRATION

Butterflies are fun to watch as they flutter around—and they are even more fun to watch when you know where they are going. Migrating butterflies travel in opposite directions during the spring and fall. If during the spring or fall you see them flying in a different direction, they may be looking for a plant from which to get nectar—their energy drink.

REARING BUTTERFLIES

A painted lady butterfly

Rearing butterflies is an enjoyable activity for scientists of all ages. The best way to get started is to purchase a "live butterfly kit" that contains larvae on artificial diet and instructions for rearing the butterflies. To rear multiple generations, you will need artificial diet or host plants. Remember to keep accurate records at each step of the process.

MATERIALS

- Live butterfly kit
- Paper towels
- Scissors
- Pop-up butterfly cage
- Straight pins
- Your field notebook
- Pencil

STEP 1: Search online for "painted lady butterflies for sale" and contact the vendor nearest where you live. Purchase a kit and enough extra artificial diet to rear an additional dozen larvae.

STEP 2: When your kit arrives, open each cup and examine the larvae (fig. 1).

STEP 3: Cut out round pieces of paper towel slightly larger than the cup's opening. Place 1 piece over each diet cup with larvae and snap on the lid holding the paper in place.

STEP 4: Monitor the larvae's growth: When they have grown to the proper size they will climb to the top of the cup and use silk to attach to the paper towel (fig. 2). When their body forms a "J" shape they will soon form a chrysalis and metamorphosis is about to happen in about 2 weeks.

Fig. 1: Examine the larvae in your artificial diet cups.

Fig. 2: Once they reach proper size, the larvae climb to the top and use silk to attach to the paper towel.

Fig. 3: When the chrysalises form, attach the paper with the chrysalises using straight pins to the top of the pop-up butterfly cage so they hang vertically.

STEP 5: When the chrysalis forms, remove the paper with the chrysalis and use a straight pin to attach the paper to the top of the pop-up butterfly cage so the chrysalis hangs vertically (fig. 3). This position mimics its position in nature and is important for the metamorphosis that is taking place inside.

STEP 6: After a species-specific time in their chrysalises, the butterflies emerge (fig. 4).

STEP 7: If you keep the adults in a pop-up cage with sports drink poured in a dish with a small sponge in it, they will quickly begin to breed and produce eggs! Place paper towels in the bottom of the cage for them to lay eggs on.

STEP 8: When the eggs hatch and very small caterpillars start crawling around (fig. 5), transfer them to the extra diet cups you purchased. When this second group emerges you can stage a butterfly release!

Fig. 4: When the time is right, the butterflies emerge!

Fig. 5: Painted lady butterfly eggs and larvae

BUG SCIENCE

Many entomologists rear arthropods for research and education. Many companies around the world rear insects for pollination and pest control, research, and food. Most rearing facilities that rear butterflies for release purchase artificial diet.

CARDINAL DIRECTIONS & MONARCHS' MIGRATION

MATERIALS

- **Compass or smartphone compass app**
- **Your field notebook**
- **Pencil**

STEP 1: Learn your cardinal directions and either put a compass on your key ring (fig. 1) or a compass app on your smartphone (fig. 2). You will need to record the direction the butterflies are flying, such as "from south to north," in your field notebook.

STEP 2: Set up a migration table in your field notebook (see opposite), one for each species you are monitoring.

STEP 3: You may not always have your field notebook with you, so when you see monarchs or other butterflies, check their direction and number and record them on scrap paper for transcribing to your field notebook later. Monarchs are easy to identify in the form of a caterpillar, chrysalis or adult (figs. 3 and 4).

In this activity, we monitor butterfly migration. Observing a monarch's migrations helps us learn about their health and habits. The migrations are so accurate in repetition they could be used as living compasses twice a year!

BUTTERFLY MIGRATION TABLE

DATE	LOCATION	DIRECTION HEADED	NUMBER SIGHTED	PLANT INTERACTIONS

Figs. 1 and 2: Use a compass or a smartphone compass app to learn cardinal directions.

Figs. 3 and 4: Monarch caterpillars, chrysalises, and butterflies are easy to identify.

BUG SCIENCE

- Insects migrate to find suitable habitats to survive the seasons. Butterflies are some of the best known and enjoyed migrants, and there are migrations of different butterflies on several continents. The most notable migrating insects in the United States include the monarch, sulphur, and painted lady butterflies. By monitoring migrating butterflies over the years, the health of butterflies can be determined.

- There is concern that the monarch migration may be in jeopardy. The loss of habitat in Mexico and changes in land use in the United States are considered possible causes.

Like the monarch (see Lab 37, page 118), the yellow sulphur butterfly is another easy-to-spot butterfly that migrates. This activity uses a different survey technique to monitor sulphur butterfly migrations. When traveling, you can use what entomologists call a "transect survey." This involve counting butterflies that cross a line going in a particular direction, such as flying north across an east-west road in the spring, or south in the fall.

A yellow sulphur butterfly on a spider lily

MATERIALS

- **Your field notebook**
- **Pencil**
- **Compass or smartphone compass app**
- **Scrap paper**

STEP 1: Lay out a data table in your field notebook like the one shown on page 121.

STEP 2: Use your compass to determine the directions of local highways and roads to use as your points of comparison. Look for north–south routes as well as east–west routes. Record them in the Sulphur Migration Transect Survey (see opposite).

STEP 3: Observe the butterflies. Keep tallies on a separate sheet of paper for how many you see headed north or west in spring; in fall, tally those you see headed south or east. More sulphur butterflies head southeast in fall, and in spring they head northwest.

STEP 4: Transfer the total into the Sulphur Migration Transect Survey page in your field notebook.

SULPHUR MIGRATION TRANSECT SURVEY

DATE	HIGHWAY	STARTING POINT	ENDING POINT	SOUTH TO NORTH TALLY	EAST TO WEST TALLY	NORTH TO SOUTH TALLY	WEST TO EAST TALLY

BUG SCIENCE

Sulphur butterflies are easy to spot while traveling. They migrate to the southeast during the fall and the northwest during the spring. Traveling on an east–west highway in the spring, you would expect most sulphurs to cross the road from south to north. In the fall, they head south. The same for a north–south highway—crossing to the west in the spring and to the east in the fall. Scientists do not know if their numbers are falling like the monarchs', or are steady or increasing. Keeping a data table over a few years may help answer this question.

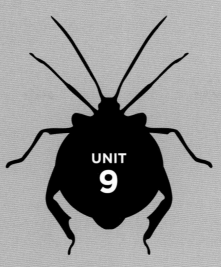

UNIT 9

BEES & OTHER POLLINATORS

Plants and insects evolved together and are dependent on each other. Insects transfer pollen from the male plants' anthers to the female plants' stigma. Without the insects' help, many plants would not bloom or produce fruit or vegetables.

Fig. 1: A scoliid wasp pollinating a yellow flower

Watch for insects (beetles, flies, ants, wasps, and butter-flies) pollinating flowers. Make a list of pollinators in your field notebook along with the plants they are pollinating. Plants have developed a symbiotic (cooperative) relationship with their pollinators so you are not likely to see a lot of different pollinators on the same plant.

MATERIALS

- **Your field notebook**
- **Pencil**
- **Field guide**
- **Camera**

STEP 1: Sketch a chart in your field notebook as shown on page 125.

STEP 2: Visit the plants in your yard or a nearby park, and begin recording the pollinators you see and the plants on which you find them (figs. 1 and 2).

STEP 3: If you do not know the plant or the pollinator, take a picture for later identification.

STEP 4: At the end of each season, total the number of pollinators in each order: Coleoptera, Diptera, Hymenoptera, and Lepidoptera.

- Which does your data suggest was the most common pollinator?

- Which plant was visited by insects from the most orders?

- Record your findings in your field notebook.

DATE	LOCATION	POLLINATOR(S)	PLANT VISITED

Fig. 2: Beetle on a daisy

BUG SCIENCE

Many insects engage in pollinating flowers and other plants. The more different types of plants you inspect, the greater variety of pollinators you will find. Honeybees are even transported great distances to pollinate crops because of the lack of enough local pollinators.

Commercial transportation of honeybees helps move them to areas that lack enough local pollinators.

Fig. 1: A honeybee on a flower

In this activity, we begin to learn about the many bees involved in pollination.

MATERIALS

- **Your field notebook**
- **Pencil**
- **Field guide**
- **Camera**

STEP 1: Make a chart like the one on page 127 in your field notebook to record the bees you observe.

STEP 2: When you're outside, be observant and begin recording the bees you see and the plants on which you find them, like a honeybee, or a carpenter bee on milkweed (figs. 1 and 2).

STEP 3: If you do not know the plant or the bee, take a picture for later identification. Maybe it's a bumblebee (fig. 3)?

STEP 4: At the end of the season, rank the different species of bees you have encountered. How many were in yards versus pollinating a home garden?

DATE	LOCATION	BEE	PLANT

Fig. 2: A carpenter bee on milkweed

Fig. 3: A bumblebee

BUG SCIENCE

There are more than 4,000 bee species in the United States alone, and field guides are available to introduce you to a large number of the more common ones. Carpenter bees, for example, can be found worldwide.

A young beekeeper gathering honey

Honey's taste and color are determined by the plants from which bees collect the nectar. Often, honeys are a blend of different types. In smaller markets and roadside stands, though, you often find honey labeled with the name of the plant the bees visited to create it. Beekeepers produce specialty honeys by placing hives with empty cone near the trees from which they wish the bees to make honey.

MATERIALS

- **Several kinds of plant-specific honeys, such as clover, lavender, orange blossom, etc.**
- **Toothpicks**
- **Your field notebook**
- **Pencil**
- **Napkins**

STEP 1: Gather several kinds of honey with a plant name (fig. 1).

STEP 2: Sample each by inserting a toothpick and tasting it (fig. 2). When you pull the toothpick out of the honey, twist it back and forth all the way to your mouth to prevent it from dripping. Discard the toothpick after sampling each honey—no double dipping to prevent contaminating the honey.

Fig. 1: Gather a variety of honeys made from different flowers and plants.

BUG SCIENCE

Nectar gives honey its flavor, and nectars from different plants taste different. Most honey purchased at grocery stores is a blend of many different kinds. Look for honey that bears the name of a plant: tupelo, sourwood, orange blossom, locust, buckwheat, clover, goldenrod, etc. This honey is produced from bees primarily visiting one kind of plant.

STEP 3: Rank the honeys you taste. Give the first sample you taste a number in the middle of the number of honeys you have. For example, give it a 5 if you have 10 honeys to sample. If the next sample tastes better give it a 4. Continue until your find your favorite, a 1, and least favorite, a 10, or the number of honeys you have.

STEP 4: Do a taste test with your family and friends and keep accurate records of their rankings in your field notebook. What is the most popular honey among your friends and family?

Fig. 2: Sampling honey

DO THE WAGGLE AND ROUND DANCES

This bee will soon be dancing to tell his friends where to find food!

Austrian scientist Karl von Frisch (1886–1982) received a Nobel Prize in 1973 for discovering how bees use the angle between the sun and the food source, including the side of the sun the food is on, to choreograph dances to communicate the location of good food sources. Get your dancing shoes on!

MATERIALS

- **Small bag of cheese puffs** (they're messy like pollen)
- **Fruit-flavored candies**
- **Group of friends to help**
- **Your field notebook**
- **Pencil**

BUG SCIENCE

Bees have an incredible way of communicating with each other—they use different dances, depending on the distance to the best nectar.

- For a food source less than 330 feet (100 m) away, bees use a "round dance."

- The better known "waggle dance" is for food between one-half mile and one mile (0.8 to 1.6 km) from the colony.

- They also bring back samples of the nectar and pollen for the other bees to try.

Waggle Dance: Food is ½ to 1 mile (0.8 to 1.6 km) away

Round Dance: Food is <660 feet (200 m) away

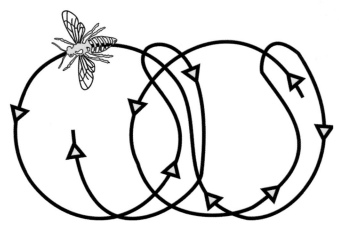

Angle from Sun

Fig. 1: The "steps" for the waggle dance

Fig. 2: The "steps" for the round dance

WAGGLE DANCE

STEP 1: Go outside on a day you can see the location of the sun. (Remember: Do not look directly at the sun.) Pick out a tree or flower *on the right side of the sun*. Estimate the angle between the sun and the flower (fig. 1).

STEP 2: Go inside and hide a bag of cheese puffs where the flowers would be in the room—first open the bag and remove a few to keep with you. Bees pass samples of the pollen (you'll use the puffs!) and the nectar (the candies) to the other workers to let them know the taste and smell of the flowers. Do not tell your friends in the room which flowers you looked at or where they are.

STEP 3: Standing in the middle of the room, identify a lamp to represent the sun. Locate a point on the wall *to the right of the lamp* about the same angle away that the flowers were to the right of the sun. Give your helpers some puffs (pollen) and candy (nectar) as you do your dance.

STEP 4: Begin by walking—waggling back and forth—toward the place on the wall *to the right of the lamp (the sun)* where the plants are (fig. 1). After 5 or 6 steps, *turn to the right* and walk back to where you started *without waggling*. Waggle in the direction of the plants again and, after 5 or 6 steps, *turn to the left* and return to your starting point *without waggling*. Do a couple more dance rounds.

STEP 5: Now it is time to go outside with your friends and see if they can find the flowers you observed as potential pollen or nectar sources. Record your results in your field notebook.

ROUND DANCE

STEP 1: Start off making a circle to the left.

STEP 2: When you return to the left of your starting point you will cross your path to the right and descend before moving back up and crossing your original path to the left (fig. 2).

STEP 3: Repeat the pattern.

Beehives are familiar sights, but native bees that conduct a huge amount of pollination are not so well known. And, native pollinators need places to live. They can be encouraged to stay close by if you build a wall in which they can live. This helps you get to know some of the native pollinators, as we do in this activity.

MATERIALS

- **Few handfuls of bamboo, 6 to 8 inches (15 to 20 cm) long, with holes ranging from 3/32 inch to 5/16 inch (3 to 8 mm)**
- **Drill (optional)**
- **Twine**
- **Scissors**
- **Clean empty soup can**
- **Your field notebook**
- **Pencil**

STEP 1: Gather the bamboo (fig. 1). Alternatively, use twigs with pithy centers, such as box elder, elderberry, raspberry, sumac, bamboo, or other twigs. Make sure one end of each cane is open. If you use twigs, drill into their pithy core to make them more attractive to the bees.

STEP 2: Bundle and tie the bamboo together (fig. 2). Place it in an empty soup can to hold it together.

STEP 3: Place the bundle in a location outside where it will be somewhat protected, like in the crotch of a tree or in a concrete block along a fence.

STEP 4: Once bees begin to move in (fig. 3), identify them and use the internet to learn what their host plants are. Plant some in your yard if you are able, or identify the plants in a nearby park.

STEP 5: Keep a record in your field notebook of your native pollinator attractor efforts.

Some wood-nesting bees build their nests in holes. As shown here, they need different sizes of holes and different sizes of canes.

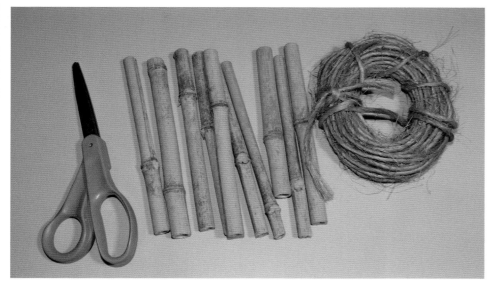

Fig. 1: Some of the basic supplies for starting a pollinator wall

Fig. 2: Bundle and tie your bamboo.

BUG SCIENCE

Honeybees were brought to America by early settlers familiar with beekeeping. America already had native pollinators, and they are enjoyable to get to know. They are not useful for honey production, but they provide pollination services for native plants and others. Native bees will scour the neighborhood in search of the nectar and pollen they need. There are about 4,000 native solitary wood-nesting bees in the United States, of which about 30 percent build nests in holes.

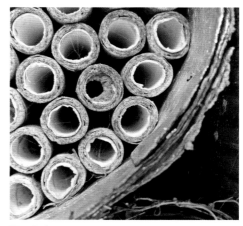

Fig. 3: An occupied habitat

EXTRAS

INSECT SAMPLING BOARD (SEE LAB 25, PAGE 88)

Key:  Coleoptera  Lepidoptera Diptera  Hymenoptera

**PITCHER PLANT TEMPLATE
(SEE LAB 34, PAGE 110)**

RESOURCES

BOOKS

National Wildlife Federation Field Guide to Insects and Spiders of North America by Arthur V. Evans

Tracks & Sign of Insects and Other Invertebrates: A Guide to North American Species by Noah Charney and Charley Eiseman

Charlotte's Web by E. B. White
An excellent book for young entomologists. The author did his homework on spiders before writing the book.

The Curious World of Bugs by Daniel Marlos

Life on a Little-Known Planet by Howard Ensign Evans

Any books by Ross E. Hutchins (These are old but outstanding and available online.)

Many states' extension services have 4-H entomology programs and their entomology manuals are online.

EDUCATION AND EVENTS

Monarch Watch
A network of teachers, volunteers, and students who are actively monitoring and conducting research involving monarchs and their migrations. They offer workshops, tag monarchs, publish monarch news, monitor population size, and dispense milkweed seed.

www.monarchwatch.org

BugFest
Check if your state hosts a BugFest or bug carnival. An extension entomologist in your state's extension service will know.

Bug & Plant Camp
The Mississippi State University's extension service runs an intergenerational, academic residential program during the summer.
ce.extension.msstate.edu/programs/summer-camps

The Boy Scouts of America
This group offers an Insect Study merit badge.

SOURCES FOR ARTHROPOD COLLECTING AND REARING SUPPLIES

Pet Stores
Some sell live arthropods.

BioQuip Products
www.bioquip.com

Carolina Biological
www.carolina.com

TAXONOMY OR NOMENCLATURE

Insects are the most abundant arthropods, but what are arthropods? This is an abbreviated classification scheme to put a few terms into perspective.

Kingdom Animalia—All animals in this book are in the Animalia with us!

  Phylum Arthropod—Most of the following are incorporated into this book

    Class Insecta

      Order Hymenoptera—1 of around 30 orders

        Family Apidae—Insects are arranged by families under each order in a collection

          Genus Apis—The first part of a two-word scientific name of an animal or insect

            Species—mellifera—The second part of the scientific name of an insect or other animal

  Class Arachnida (ticks, mites, spiders, scorpions)

  Class Diplopoda (millipedes)

  Class Chilopoda (centipedes)

  Class Malacostraca (sowbugs, pillbugs)

Bee: *Apis mellifera*

Bess beetle: *Odontotaenius disjunctus*

Black and yellow garden spider: *Argiope aurantia*

Black widow: *Latrodectus mactans*

Blister beetle: *Brachimus* spp.

Brazilian wandering spider: *Phoneutria* spp.

Brown recluse: *Loxosceles reclusa*

Brown widow: *Latrodectus geometricus*

Caddisfly: *Macrostemun zebratum*

Chilean recluse spiders in South America: *Loxosceles laeta*

Cockroach: *Periplaneta americana*

Crane fly: *Trichocera* spp.

Damselfly: *Enallagma civile*

Dermestid beetle: *Dermestidae* spp.

Eastern tiger swallowtail: *Papilio glaucus*

Funnel-web spider: *Hadronyche modesta* in Australia, New Zealand, and Southeast Asia

Grandaddy longlegs: *Leibonum rotundum*

Green lacewing: *Chrysopa* or *Chrysoperla* spp.

Hercules beetle: *Dynastes tityus*

Horsefly: *Tabanus quinquevittatus*

Kissing bug: *Triatominae* spp.

Leaf-footed bug: *Coreus* spp.

Mealworm: *Tenebrio molitor*

Milkweed bug: *Oncopeltus fasciatus*

Millipede: *Apheloria virginiensis*

Monarch butterfly: *Danaus plexippus*

Moth: *Eacles imperialis*

Painted lady butterfly: *Vanessa cardui*

Paper wasp: *Polistes aurifer*

Pillbug: *Armadillidium vulgare*

Potter wasp: *Eumenes fraternus*

Redback spider: *Latrodectus hasseltii* in Australia, New Zealand, and Southeast Asia

Redheaded centipede: *Scolopendra* sp.

Robber fly: *Diogmites* spp.

Six-eyed sand spider in Africa: *Sicarius hahni*

Sow bug: *Porcellio scaber*

Stag beetle: *Dorcus parallelus*

Stink bug: *Nezara viridula*

Termite—Isoptora: *Reticulitermes, Coptotermes, Incisitermes* etc.

Wheel bug: *Arilus cristatus*

Wolf spider: *Rabidosa rabida*

Yellow jacket: *Vespula* or *Dolichovespula* spp.

Yellow sac spider in many countries: *Cheiracanthium* spp.

ACKNOWLEDGMENTS

I would like to express my great appreciation to Dr. Mike Williams for persisting in getting me involved in Bug Camp, and to the campers whose curiosity has been an ongoing inspiration. The Biochemistry, Molecular Biology, Entomology, and Plant Pathology Department at Mississippi State University has provided the opportunity and facilities for developing a next-generation camp. The Entomological Society of America and their Education and Outreach Committee have been my professional home and inspiration for young campers, including Breanna Lyle, Matthew Thorn, and others.

ABOUT THE AUTHOR

Dr. John Guyton is an Extension Entomologist in the Biochemistry, Molecular Biology, Entomology, and Plant Pathology Department at Mississippi State University. He was a science educator at Murray State University in Kentucky and participated in writing the science portion of the first state-mandated curriculum framework. His diverse background and leadership of numerous projects have earned him a commission as a Kentucky Colonel, the American Horticulture Society's Great American Gardener Educator of the Year, and Project Learning Tree's Outstanding Educator of the Year awards. Two U. S. Fish and Wildlife directors have presented Guyton with Regional Directors' Honor Awards for Volunteer Service. The Mississippi legislature has recognized his efforts with two legislative resolutions.

This Eagle Scout describes himself as a lifelong adventurer, leading his Explorer Post on a 355-mile (571 km) canoe trip while in high school, chasing total solar eclipses from Canada deep into Mexico, SCUBA diving, parasailing, climbing the Pyramid to the Sun, and leading intense intergenerational academic Bug and Plant Camps.

INDEX